MECHANICS-
MERCANTILE
LIBRARY.

Arthur F. Mathews '06

*Grief*

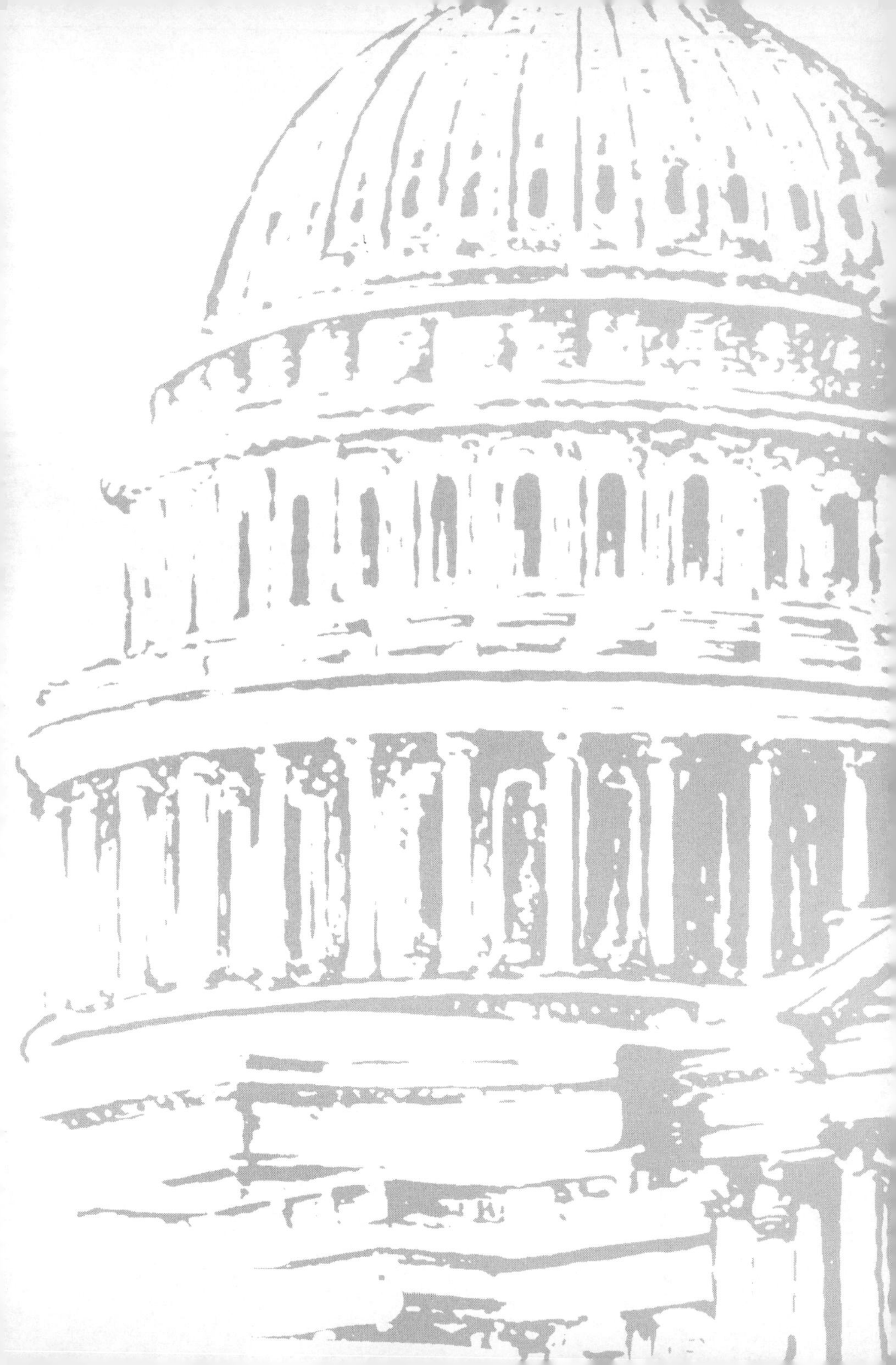

# GRIEF

## Andrew Holleran

———◆———

HYPERION

NEW YORK

This book is a work of fiction; names,
characters, and incidents are either products of the author's
imagination or are used fictitiously. Any resemblance to actual
events or persons, living or dead, is entirely coincidental.

LIBRARY OF CONGRESS CATALOGING-IN-PUBLICATION DATA

Holleran, Andrew.
Grief / Andrew Holleran.—1st ed.
p.   cm.
ISBN 1-4013-0250-5
1. College teachers—Fiction.   2. Parents—Death—Fiction.
3. Loss (Psychology)—Fiction.   4. Washington (D.C.)—Fiction.
5. Widowers—Fiction.   I. Title.
PS3558.O3496G75   2006
813'.54—dc22                          2005045627

Hyperion books are available for special promotions and
premiums. For details contact Michael Rentas, Assistant
Director, Inventory Operations, Hyperion,
77 West 66th Street, 12th floor, New York, New York 10023,
or call 212-456-0133.

*Book design by Fritz Metsch*

FIRST EDITION

1   3   5   7   9   10   8   6   4   2

*Grief*

THE HOUSE I lived in that winter in Washington had been a rooming house with fourteen rooms, rented out mostly to addicts, when my landlord bought it in 1974. Friends told him it was a bad idea, but he bought it anyway, and his father came from Alabama to help rebuild the interior from the ground up. As soon as he could, he rented the basement apartment. The bedroom on the top floor he rented from time to time. The rest of the house was his. It was one of those row houses people walk by on fall nights and stop beside to look at the architectural details, the molding, the chandeliers, the bookcases, visible through the tall windows, while straining for glimpses of life within. Often when they did this my landlord was sitting there in the dark in the front room with his dog on his lap, looking down into the street. He would sit there thinking of the nights he used to look at houses like his, enjoying the reversal of roles, till he realized his upstairs tenant was coming up the front steps—when I would see him stand up, gather the dog to his chest, and bolt to his study—the nicest room in the house, with a bay window on the second floor, and a spacious desk, and all his books and papers.

The weekend I arrived, however, my landlord wasn't home; he was at another house he owned, in the mountains, three hours west of the city, where he had a small shop that sold a mix of antiques, theatrical props, and novelties. It was the holiday honoring Martin Luther King Jr. The airports were so empty it felt like I was passing through Limbo—from one life to the next. In fact I was leaving behind a life: the non-life, rather, that people who take care of someone face after the invalid dies; in this case, after a long period of helplessness spent mostly in a nursing home—a place that my mother had always asked me to keep her out of, no matter what happened; till what happened made it necessary. The idea of moving to a city seemed like a good idea, so when an old friend asked me if I'd teach a course—someone was going on sabbatical—I accepted.

But sitting in the airport on a Saturday I had only felt lost. Like someone cleaning a room who opens a drawer and finds something he did not want to find, I realized I had chosen to travel on the one day when I felt worst; since Saturday was the day when I had for the past twelve years driven to the nursing home to remove my mother for the weekend—a day of such happiness for both of us (eliminating the nursing home), that the only thing that spoiled it was the gauntlet of people who were being left behind when I wheeled her chair down the hallway, a prisoner being freed while the others watched. Or perhaps, I thought now, that was an element of the pleasure; so confused was I still about what all that had meant. What was clear was that I'd become used to going there on Saturdays; something I was not doing among the strangers sitting around me in the vacant sunny lounge of the airport in Atlanta—that womb, that amniotic fluid, in which the traveler floats, detached from all his elements of identity. To get to Heaven, the joke goes, you change planes in Atlanta. The day my mother had fallen I'd flown north as if going to the afterlife, traveling toward what I thought was her death as in a dream, too much in shock to even feel anything but strange; the silence of the cabin, the clouds outside, the quiet passengers, all ignorant of my awful news. Now, after her death, years later, I was flying north again with the same bizarre feeling. You never know, I thought, watching the other passengers settle into the plastic chairs around me, who is flying on a bereavement discount. There's no way to tell—though most of the families I could see, peering over the newspaper I was reading at their exchanges, seemed to still have one another.

I was the solitary traveler this time; on a day whose future identity had been my own selfish worry when my mother died: What would I do with each Saturday? How would I get up that morning knowing there was no need to get in the car to drive into the nursing home to take her out? It was only now that the dimensions of the routine we had established were becoming clear. "It's the families who keep the patient alive," a nurse had said to me one day in the nursing home. "They're the ones who won't let go." Nurses are the supreme realists, I thought as I sat in the vacant anonymity of an airport on a weekend when very few people seemed to be traveling. It's in airports that we feel most lost; in airports that we grieve. So when I got to Washington I went outside to get the Metro with a feeling that I was breathing for the first time in hours.

The weather the day I showed up was neither warm nor cold. The keys had been mailed a week earlier; a note welcoming me was on the table in the entrance hall—and for the next two days I had the place to myself.

Not only the house, but the neighborhood itself, was empty. Happy to be starting over, however, I began to walk. Years earlier a friend who'd lived in Washington had said when asked why he'd left: "I refused to go to one more dinner party where people talked about their town houses as if they were children." But I could see, only hours after arriving there that January afternoon, on my first exploration of the neighborhood, how this could happen. Everywhere I looked I saw row houses. Unlike those in Manhattan, they exhibited a great variation in design. There was something Germanic about them: little castles. Turrets and towers marked the corners in every direction, conical roofs of black slate, with dormer windows that looked like half-opened eyes gazing out between the chimneys and balconies. Though smaller than Manhattan brownstones, and composed of different colored stone, they presented the onlooker with the same reassuring sense of comfort and solidity, as if you were walking through a novel by William Dean Howells or Henry James.

This feeling only deepened that first afternoon when I unlocked the door at the top of the stairs and found myself looking through a window into the study of the house next door, a nook filled with bookcases, African violets, and an elderly couple on a small sofa engaged in what looked like a perpetual conversation. On the landing outside were a few clay pots still holding the remains of summer—dried stalks of basil and rosemary. The iron gate I had to unlatch, before opening the old wooden door, implied there was crime about, but once I opened it, and the inner door in the entrance hall, I felt quite safe—plunged into the silvery, aqueous gloom of the house itself: a gray light provided by two glass doors in the back, which gave onto a wooden deck whose stairs led down to a narrow brick-walled garden lined with tall fir trees. The firs made the garden look Nordic. The décor inside the house was strictly American, however—banquettes, spot lighting, and gray walls—the furniture eclectic: a fine chair upholstered in striped gold and silver, next to a plastic table with a lava lamp, a big rococo mirror that leaned against one wall, and, against the wall opposite, one of those dead-white sculptures nineteenth-century America considered masterpieces but this century regards as kitsch—in this case, according to the thick letters raised on its pediment, *Boy with a Thorn.*

The youth removing a thorn from his foot was illumined by a spotlight in the ceiling I tried to turn off by flicking the switches on a panel beside it; but touching the switches only turned every light on in various sections of the ground floor, which made me think: *Lighting is what the seventies were all about.* It was all like a house someone had designed in 1978—a more hedonistic era poured into the walls of this deep, narrow, sober old building, where, that first evening, I found myself sitting in the dark looking down into the twilight where two men in jeans and plaid shirts were washing a car. I could not decide if the fact that I was able to wander at will that first weekend was welcoming or cold; especially when, while looking for clues to my landlord's life, I found none. *Go ahead, look,* the house seemed to say—*you won't find a thing about me here.*

But this seemed appropriate. As I walked through the house I felt like a ghost myself, or like someone turning the pages in a back issue of *Architectural Digest*—to which, despite its do-it-yourself homeliness, the house seemed to aspire. In the dining room hung a large painting that looked as if someone had copied Caravaggio, not very well; this knockoff was not much more effective than the handle of the washer and dryer in the alcove off the kitchen that came off in my hand. There were drawers that didn't open, lights that didn't work. In the cabinet above the stove were only a rusted can of paprika and one small jar of peanut butter. It was as if no one had ever eaten there. The house was a sort of tomb that first weekend. The more I looked the emptier it seemed, and when I caught my reflection accidentally in the enormous mirror leaning against the wall of the living room it brought me to a halt—the pale silvery figure staring back at me looked so tentative and sad.

When I finally climbed the stairs to my bedroom on the third floor, I lay down on the big low bed and stared at the single strand of ivy that had climbed to the top of a brick wall behind the house, and, beyond it, more rooftops and a building under construction. I was glad to be alone and at the same time apprehensive. When I turned on the lamp beside the bed the room looked like a hotel room in a strange city.

On the table by the bed were three books standing upright between two glass clowns that served as bookends— a murder mystery by Ruth Rendell, a book about Elizabeth Nietzsche's Aryan colony in Paraguay, and *Mary Todd Lincoln: Her Life and Letters*, by Justin and Linda Levitt Turner.

I opened the middle book and looked at the pictures of Nietzsche's sister, and the handsome men with big moustaches who had followed her to Paraguay, standing next to a cart on a dirt road in the jungle. Then rain started pattering on the skylight above the landing and I fell asleep.

WHEN I AWOKE I picked up the letters of Mary Todd Lincoln—which proved to be so engrossing that as I lay there reading that first night in Washington it took me a few seconds to make sure I'd heard the doorbell before going down to investigate.

When I got to the front door a slender black man in a soiled windbreaker was tapping on the front window as he leaned sideways from the landing. I opened the doors and said hello. He said he knew my landlord, lived a few doors down the street, had just been in an accident in Dupont Circle, his wife was in George Washington University Hospital, and he needed ninety dollars to get his car, which had been towed away. I decided it would be racist to doubt his word—so I gave him what money I had and closed the door. Moments later the doorbell rang again. This time it was a white man who introduced himself as the downstairs tenant and asked if the man who had just come to the door had asked for money because he'd been in a car accident.

"Yes," I said, "he said he's a neighbor and knows our landlord."

The man emitted a short laugh.

"He lives on a bench in Dupont Circle and there was no car accident. How much did you give him?"

"Twenty bucks," I said.

"Well, you didn't know," he said, turning to walk down the stairs. "And it *is* Martin Luther King's birthday. I guess you could call it—reparations!" Then he laughed, and disappeared beneath the stairs to his apartment.

Outside another stranger—a weathered, handsome man in blue jeans and a plaid coat—was bent over at the waist, picking leaves off the sidewalk in the lamplight one by one and putting them in his pocket. When I put on my coat and went out, he neither spoke nor looked at me. After living alone in a small town I had lost the knowledge of how to pass people on the street: whether to look at them—and for how long—whether or not to nod or say hello.

One of the odd aspects of caring for someone for a long time is that you grow accustomed to a certain intimacy—but as I walked down the dark, tree-lined block, past house after house just like my landlord's, with lamps burning within, and pots of dead flowers on the stoops, I realized I belonged to no one now, and no one belonged to me. I was like a crab that has shed one shell but not found another; and when I returned from the grocery store, I did what a crustacean must do when it finds a new carapace to occupy: resume its old habits—unpacked the groceries, searched for the classical radio station, and sat down to read the newspaper while they played an oboe concerto by Mozart. Outside the front door lay not the small town in which I'd been living but a city with bars, restaurants, and concert halls, but they made no difference; I had merely changed the room in which I sat and the newspaper I was reading.

I was reading a story on the front page about the recent brouhaha in the municipal government in which the new African-American mayor had fired a white man who had used the word "niggardly" during a budget meeting. A black aide had stormed out of the meeting claiming he had been insulted. The homosexual community was calling on the mayor to rehire the white aide, who was gay, because the word "niggardly" was an old English term that had nothing to do with race. One columnist was arguing that a white person should have known that whatever its meaning this word could give offense. A letter to the editor argued that white people should not have to bow to the lexical deficiencies of blacks. A second article claimed the black aide's outrage was bogus and had been staged by a cabal of civil servants who felt threatened by the new regime; a permanent bureaucracy that was against all reform because it felt any change would simply allow whites to take over the city.

I was reading still another installment in this ongoing story at the dining room table on Monday when my landlord came through the door. "Hi!" he said, as he put down his duffel bag, and a small brown and white dog walked toward me, its toenails clicking on the floor. "Biscuit! Come here!" he called. The dog stopped in its tracks, looking at me with bright eyes. Then he said: "Welcome to Washington! Nice to see you!"

I stood up, shook his hand, and apologized for having been so absorbed in the story in the *Post* about the mayor that I'd not heard him come in. He returned to a table on which I'd put the mail. "Oh, please," he said, picking up the envelopes. "I don't know if you've been out and around yet, but if you have, you may have noticed a lot of subtle, and not so subtle, racial hostility in this town. People like me, the ones who marched in all the civil rights marches in the sixties, have become very discouraged. *Very* discouraged," he said, as he began opening the envelopes. "Most of us who were behind civil rights from the beginning have just about given up on the whole thing. I won't even try to sit down next to a black person on the Metro because I know if I do that person will not move an inch to make space for me—not even half an inch! You'll see. There's a subtext to life in this city, an unspoken comment that accompanies almost every exchange, which is: 'You stupid white man.' But here I am on my soapbox already and all I wanted to say was welcome to Washington! Come here, Biscuit!" he said to the little dog sniffing at my ankles.

I was looking at a man my age in green corduroy pants, a blue buttoned-down shirt, and a navy blue parka. He had thick salt and pepper hair cut short, and—curious anachronism—a neat moustache. His eyes were small and deep set. Two creases formed parentheses around a thin mouth. It was the sort of face that had been used in the seventies to advertise cigarettes. He was probably better-looking now than he had been in his youth, though the expression on his face implied that his looks had not brought him peace of mind—there was a certain discontent, an unease, visible in the way he moved two fingers back and forth nervously across his neat moustache while reading the envelope in his left hand. He looked a little like John Brown, the Abolitionist, it occurred to me. Then he glanced up. "Is your room all right?" he said.

"Very nice," I said.

"You know, I still get letters for people who haven't lived here in ten years," he said as he tossed envelopes into the wastebasket, and then went on to tell me who these previous tenants were: an actor who'd had a dog of his own that pooped all over the place; a student who'd gone on to get a job with the phone company in Seattle; a clarinetist who'd played at the White House when in the Marines; a soldier named Leonard Matlovich who'd been discharged by the Air Force for being homosexual and who was now buried not far from J. Edgar Hoover in the Congressional Cemetery on Capitol Hill (a juxtaposition my landlord liked). Though he was proud that Matlovich had lived here, and extremely amiable at that moment, watching the letters being tossed into the wastebasket, I got an odd sense that he'd grown used to having the house to himself. I was only there as a favor to the mutual friend who'd asked him if I could rent a room, I concluded, and, of course, provide a monthly check; but that was all. Nevertheless I insisted he share my dinner. "Oh no, I couldn't," he said, and went into the kitchen and began assembling his own. "I always buy a ton of chicken parts and boil them all at once, so I can live on them for a month and always have something to eat." When he was done arranging some of these on a tray, like something one takes an invalid, he called the little dog, and began going upstairs.

When he was halfway up I remembered to tell him a young man had knocked on the door and asked for money because of an auto accident in Dupont Circle that had sent his wife to the hospital. "Oh," he said, coming to a stop, "never do that, The Circle used to be a big drug bazaar. People are always working some scam. There's a woman with five kids who pushes a stroller down the street. She'll ask you for something too. She's been doing it so long you'd think her kids should be in college now. I think she just borrows new ones. Then there's the drunk with all her teeth missing and tears streaming down her face. You'll probably run into her." Then I mentioned the downstairs tenant who'd knocked on the door. He said, "That's Jim. His mother died and left him a lot of money. He doesn't have to work. He just goes to museums. He has a boyfriend he keeps hidden away so ogres like me can't corrupt him." Finally, when I asked who the man was I'd seen picking up leaves one by one and putting them in his pocket, he laughed. "Oh," he said. "He's a Vietnam vet the block hired to keep things clean, who's not quite all there. Welcome to Mister Rogers' neighborhood!" he said, and continued upstairs.

*So*, I thought, *we are both used to living alone. We have our habits, our little ruts.* Moments later I extinguished the downstairs lights and went up past the two closed doors of his study on the second floor to my own room on the third, and lay down on the big low bed to listen to the rain on the skylight above the landing; a pleasant sound that was the last thing I heard on my first evening in that house with my landlord, whose bonhomie had made me feel even lonelier than before. Well, I thought, thinking of Lincoln when he rode the judicial circuit and slept five to a bed in taverns along the way, that's America—still a big boardinghouse.

IN FACT THE first letter from his wife to Lincoln in the book I'd found by the bed had been sent to a boardinghouse in Washington on Capitol Hill, where Lincoln was living as a congressman. Even this one gave me her style ("You will think indeed, that *old age*, has set *its seal*, upon my humble self, that in few or none of my letters, I can remember the day of the month, I must confess it as one of my peculiarities; I feel wearied & tired enough to know, that this is *Saturday night*, our *babies* are asleep . . .")—a style that made it easy the next day to remain upstairs in my room reading till I was sure my landlord had left the house. Only then did I go downstairs. As I was reading more of the letters at breakfast—letters written when she was happy, when everyone was still alive—the doorbell rang. A man in a UPS uniform was at the door; I told him I was not the person he was looking for, but when he said he'd have to take the shipment back if no one signed for it, I forged my landlord's name, thinking: *He'll be glad I was here to do this.* Then I left the boxes in the hall and walked across Dupont Circle to see the friend who'd asked me to take the place of his colleague on leave.

Frank lived in an old apartment building on Sixteenth Street, where he had been since the seventies, when, he told me, the place was full of illegal Central American immigrants, who, when the owners decided to convert the building to a condominium, had no legal recourse and fled. The street had been shabby then, he said, another casualty of the riots in 1968 from which the city was still recovering; but now Sixteenth Street was lined with refurbished apartment buildings whose gothic traceries and formal porticoes looked fairly grand under the tall trees. He met me at his door in a red robe—a big man with beautiful blue eyes and blond bangs who looked like the Little Dutch Boy that used to be on the cans of paint, though these blue eyes held a light that was as challenging as it was cheerful. Retying the belt, he led me back to his bedroom and lay down beneath a large crucifix on the wall, where the impression he gave of blooming health, of big hearty brightness, faded as he took a cigarette from the pack on the table by his bed, lighted it, and said: "Forgive me, I'm not feeling well. But I'm so glad you're here. Are you settled in? Is the house all right?"

"Beautiful," I said. "I've never lived in a house like that before."

"Few people have," he said. "It's a luxury—to have a house in D.C. Or anywhere for that matter. I was so relieved he said yes when I asked if you could. I wasn't sure he'd want to rent. But I think the prospect of six fifty a month, which is quite cheap really, turned the tide. I'm glad you like it. Now—school. You start next Thursday. Just drive out with me, and I'll introduce you to everyone and get you your desk. Now—me. Do you want to go with me and the Lug to the movies tonight at seven?"

"Who's the Lug?" I said.

"My boyfriend," he said. "I can't decide if he's God's reward for all my suffering the past few years, or a demon sent straight from Hell to drive me out of my mind. Perhaps you can tell me if you go with us to the moving pictures. Would you?"

Having read of a chamber music concert at the Society of the Cincinnati—a mansion on Massachusetts Avenue I'd noticed near my landlord's—I asked my friend if he wouldn't rather do that.

"No," he said, "I need a big, explosive, action-packed movie—I want to see Keanu Reeves blow things up. So I'll pass. In the meantime, sit down. How do I look?"

"Wonderful," I said.

"Do you notice the swelling?" he said.

"Where?" I said.

"My stomach," he said. "I've had a terrible day."

He'd had a terrible decade: having cared for, then buried, a lover, he'd nearly died after being diagnosed with cancer. Then, six months after the operation excising that, he had buried his mother—confined to a nursing home in Chicago the previous eight years; a fact I was reminded of when he suddenly said, in a strangely altered voice, as I sat down on the edge of the bed: "Could you just fluff my pillow first? And get the cold cream? I find cold cream so soothing on a day like this one!"

"I don't see how you can joke like that," I said.

"It's easy," he said. "She didn't even recognize me the last two years. Besides, grief is useless after a certain point—don't you agree?"

"I suppose so," I said, "but everyone's point is different."

"Of course," he said, "but the sooner you get over it, the better. Because none of us has any time to waste, you know. I'm sure your mother didn't expect you to sit in that house down there for the rest of your life babysitting her figurines. You can't sit shivah forever."

"Yes, you can."

"What do you mean?"

"I mean the only cure for grief is time, but some people

need more than others—some people in fact may never have enough time. Not everyone can move on," I said.

"Why not?" he said in a cool voice.

"Because grief is what you have after someone you love dies. It's the only thing left of that person. Your love for, your missing, them. And as long as you have that, you're not alone—you have them."

"But they're gone!" he said.

"Not if you grieve," I said. "Your grief is the substitute for their presence on earth. Your grief *is* their presence on earth."

"No, it's not—because they're still not there!" he said. "Unless you believe in the afterlife. You don't believe in the afterlife, do you?"

"I'm not sure."

"I don't see how you can," he said.

"Why?"

"It raises too many questions if you do. Like: How old are you in eternity? How old are your parents? Do you have to go to the toilet? Where does everyone sit, what do you do at night? And where are they now if they still exist? I know it's hard to accept the fact that people disintegrate into a little pile of chemicals worth about sixty-seven cents on the current market, but in all likelihood that seems to be the case. So there's no point in grieving any longer than you want—or have to."

"Don't you still feel grief over your mother?"

"Not really," he said, blowing out a stream of smoke. "That may be because she no longer knew who I was when I came into the room. Or it may be because it was a question of survival—I was fighting for my own life at the time. Of course I always was, with her. Or it may be that I'm not over it yet at all, but have to focus on other things. Grief is a luxury, I think, I can't afford. One has to move on."

"But I've watched people try," I said, "and fail."

"Who?"

"I've seen a lot of friends make mistakes—they lose someone, they try to start a new life—and make one wrong choice after another."

"But what's wrong with that? You always make mistakes," he said. "How could you not?"

"But no one *wants* to make mistakes," I said. "No one does anything thinking it's going to be a mistake."

"Of course they don't," he said. "But they do *do* something. The point is to choose—something—it almost doesn't matter what. But choose! You have to start over!"

"But what is the point—of starting over? Henry Adams, after his wife killed herself, said he was too young to die, but too old to start over. That's the problem with our age."

"What does Henry Adams have to do with it?"

"I was thinking of him when the church bells were ringing as I was walking through Lafayette Square last night."

"But why?" he said.

"Because Adams had to deal with grief. He was forty-seven when his wife killed herself. She had just taken care of her own father till he died. Then she returned to Washington. Everything seemed fine. Then one day while Henry Adams was downstairs reading she went upstairs and swallowed one of the chemicals she used to develop her photographs. She left a note saying that if only she had one good quality, she would have continued living, but she didn't. Of course she had lots of good qualities—she had just nursed her father through his final illness. It was pure depression, pure guilt. Adams was devastated—but his grief took an unusual form. The day after she died, he came downstairs, tore the mourning band off his arm, and forbade anyone to mention his wife's name ever again. Nor does he even mention it in his autobiography. In contrast to Mary Todd Lincoln," I said. "Who grieved till she died—in a more ostentatious manner—who, you might say, tried to move on and couldn't."

"Because she was bipolar," said my friend, pushing his blond bangs off his forehead.

"She was a woman who was subject to a string of disasters so awful, one after the other, you can see perfectly well why she never got over them. Nothing comes close to what happened to Mary Todd Lincoln."

"What about Jackie Kennedy?" he said. "Jackie

Kennedy saw her husband shot, too. But she moved on. A second act that was *quite* dignified and productive. And do you know why?"

"Why?" I said.

"Social class," he said, stubbing out his cigarette. "I suspect it was simply social class. Of course she was also medicated."

"What does grief have to do with social class?"

"Everything!" he said. "At least it has to do with how you behave—like a Roman, or a banshee. Mary Lincoln ended up the second!"

"But there are a lot of people who never get over certain things," I said. "Something in them snaps—something that binds them to life. The past becomes their home. The dead become more real to them than the living—because there are more of the dead. They miss the dead, and when that happens, life stops."

"Speak for yourself," he said, standing up and tying the belt of his robe about him. He went to the window and looked down onto Sixteenth Street. "For me life has just begun! I'm like the woman behind the bar in a French movie stuffing francs into her bra. I'm counting every chit I get! I want it all! And that's my advice to you! I think you should buy a place in Washington," he said, turning around. "The market is never going to go down. It may level off but you won't lose money. And we can find you someone. Everyone here is so middle class, even the fags want to be married. I think you should start looking now!"

INSTEAD I RETURNED to N Street, and was still at the dining room table finishing an early supper when my landlord came home. When he entered the house I started to stand up, out of some instinct of politeness; then I stopped myself and told him I had signed for the boxes that were still in the hall. He gasped. He said he was having a dispute with the supplier of the items in the boxes—novelty clocks—and that now, by accepting them, I had weakened his case, though he told me not to worry, he would straighten it out, he might still get them to pick up the clocks by putting a stop on his credit card.

He was utterly amiable, in short, even about this mistake, which had complicated, not helped, the situation; in fact, if anything, I realized, before the evening was out, the problem was that we were both too polite. Manners are counterproductive when they make you wonder about the person's true feelings. At one point in our discussion—a dispute over which of us should use the fourth shelf of the refrigerator—he laughed and said: "Stop! We're having a politeness contest!"

When he laughed his eyes slanted upward and his face assumed a shrewd, almost devilish expression. But the laughter cleared the air—though he soon returned to the politeness that left me unable to discern his real feelings about anything, and so I kept thoughts to myself in the succeeding days. I got over the instinct to stand when he came into the dining room. Both of us made small talk with a light touch. But I felt best when I was out of the house. That was why I took long walks—in part to avoid my landlord, in part to leave behind the feeling of having been trapped in the house I'd been living in before coming here.

Most walks led to the White House: down Connecticut Avenue or Sixteenth Street, past the Jefferson Hotel—where Dick Morris had sucked the prostitute's toes—the old Russian embassy and the Hilton Hotel, the clusters of homeless men in the entryway of the Episcopal church, into Lafayette Square, where the only person was usually the woman who lived in a pup tent on its south side protesting nuclear weapons. Often at night a group of Japanese tourists was getting out of a bus taking them on a nocturnal tour of Washington, but they quickly got their pictures and vanished. That evening not even a skateboarder intervened on the dead, blocked-off stretch of Pennsylvania Avenue, however; the enormous lantern under the portico of the White House beamed brightly, and beyond the windows of the East Room, the twinkling chandeliers gave off an amber glow that was the color of a glass of expensive scotch. Five minutes after I arrived the floodlights flicked off, and the mansion was plunged into shadow, and looked suddenly sad, as if, at Lights Out, everyone inside had been sent to bed with milk and cookies. Then a policeman approached and said, "Good evening," to me, at which point I realized I'd acquired the profile of a presidential assassin, and I moved on.

The television cameras and microphones massed along the driveway to the west of the portico, left in place for the next broadcast, were shrouded in black tarpaulins against the rain, looking more than anything like a cluster of tombstones. On the eastern side there was a long narrow walk between the White House and the Treasury Building. A young waiter stood, a white jacket and black pants slung over his shoulders on hangers, talking to a man in the guardhouse, like an actor on his way home from a performance; a witness to history we would never hear from. Then, just past the monument to General Sherman, Pennsylvania Avenue resumed. All the way down the sidewalk was empty except for the homeless men sleeping in the deep shadows on benches—until the reflecting pool beneath the Capitol, where lovers had parked their cars to neck. From the terrace of the Capitol the city felt strangely hushed, like a seaport after dark, lights ringing a dark harbor—only here the harbor was not the ocean but the Mall.

When I returned to the house, I stopped across the street to look at it: suddenly somber, secretive, set slightly back, aloof, above the street at the top of its zigzagging staircase.

When you were inside you had the impression that people on the sidewalk could look in and see everything; but in fact, I realized now, the main floor was above the sight line of a pedestrian, set back from the street, reserved and demure. Once the door had closed behind me, once more in its aqueous gloom, I walked across the golden floor, careful to make no noise, and stopped to look at my reflection in the mirror—a tall, slender man in an overcoat, silver-haired, pale and indistinct. Then I turned out the lights, removed my shoes, and crept up the stairs, past the closed gray doors of my landlord's bedroom. The house was profoundly still. The next morning I again waited for him to leave for work before I went downstairs. But he startled me by having lingered at the breakfast table—a surprise I camouflaged by sitting down beside him with my bowl of oatmeal and telling him about my walk. He listened politely and told me there were several interesting things to see in our own neighborhood—Alice Roosevelt Longworth's house on Massachusetts Avenue; the house in which Woodrow Wilson had spent his last years; the mansion built by the heiress who had owned the Hope Diamond, whose life was ruined when her only son ran out onto Massachusetts Avenue and was struck by a carriage (now the jewel was in a museum on the Mall and the mansion was the Indonesian embassy). I could tell he liked history. He even went upstairs and brought back a large book called *Capital Losses*, which contained photographs of

Beaux-Arts mansions that had been torn down to make room for the office buildings that ringed the rotaries now, and left me with a Michelin Guide, which gave me an objective for the walks I began taking every day now, to see something new, to distract myself.

Many people have tried to explain Washington—it's a one-company town, or a giant cemetery, or a city of permanent blacks and transient whites, or a town people come to only to improve their résumé, or a city no one can call home because it belongs to the nation—but the best observation I came upon while crossing the plaza in front of the National Theatre where the pavement is engraved with quotations about the city. Here is what James Fenimore Cooper wrote in 1838 about the capital: "It is mean in detail, but the outline has a certain grandeur about it." That's it. There's something still halfhearted about Washington, as if the country cannot make up its mind about government itself—a city that, block by block, weaves in and out of grandeur and shabbiness. Even the grandeur is mostly indebted to the Civil War. Its generals and heroes command every circle, their names christen them, as if only war, and not government, made this a capital. It is the buildings put up in the flush of construction following the defeat of the South that are the big, important ones.

One afternoon I stumbled on Ford's Theatre. The box in which Lincoln had been shot was closed, the park ranger said, so that it might recuperate from the thousands of feet that trod through it every year. So I went down to the little museum in the basement and stared at the coat from Brooks Brothers Lincoln had been wearing when he was shot, and the blood-soaked scarf, and the gloves—all the slightly morbid memorabilia of an age when the cult of mourning was more intense, if not macabre, than it is in our own. The little pistol (so small one could rest it on the palm of one's hand) that Booth had used lay on one shelf of a glass case containing several artifacts an Asian-American man was citing in a lecture he was giving to a young married couple. "Booth was the Robert Redford of his day! So handsome, women *and* men turned to look at him in the street!" he said. Through the walls we could hear the sound of a gospel choir from Harlem giving a matinee concert while the security guard swayed in time to the music. A mother insisted her adolescent son stand against the wall where Lincoln's height was marked. "Do it for me!" she said, knowing there was no other argument that would get him to submit to this. He stood—almost as tall as Lincoln—as I leaned forward to examine the scarf on which the dark, caked blood was still visible, this relic of another world, when limbs were amputated without anesthetic, and there was horse shit in the streets, and dead people were laid out in the parlor to make sure they were really dead before burying them, and people cut pieces from the President's bloodstained coat as a souvenir, and by the time Lincoln's corpse reached New York on its long ride home to Illinois his face had begun to collapse but all they could do was dust it off, while Mary Lincoln lay upstairs in her bedroom in the White House, incommunicado, and the public that was allowed to come and go from the White House in those days cut pieces out of the carpet and curtains she had purchased for the rooms downstairs, though it was she who was accused of looting the place. That such artifacts of grief, such souvenirs of misfortune, could still transfix people was plain, however, as I circled the room while teenagers giggled, and a black man lectured a white couple about slavery, and the Asian-American guide gave out inaccurate information about Lincoln to the married couple, all agog.

There was more across the street in the house where Lincoln had been taken after the shooting—because the doctors thought he would not survive a carriage ride to the hospital over such bumpy streets. The house was set between two souvenir shops, not far from a gay bar my landlord told me offered free drinks on Thursday nights if you wore no shirt. But the parlor and the bedroom on the first floor of this rooming house were all the more moving for their being small and shabby. Down the hall was the back bedroom in which the President had been laid at a diagonal on a bed he was too big for, in a boardinghouse whose tenants had all been out that night, allowing History to coagulate in this little room, while Mrs. Lincoln went back and forth between the parlor and the bedroom, till, after she had thrown herself across the body of her husband, her son Robert was told to keep her out. The bedroom in which Lincoln had died was the sort of room a student rents in a Midwestern university town, the back room of what might have once been a farmhouse, with a slanted floor, and windows looking out onto a narrow back porch. It was here he had expired, a park ranger said.

Then the woman next to me asked: "What did Mrs. Lincoln do—when he died?"

She was taken back to the White House, crying out as she was leaving the house, "Oh my God and have I given my husband to die."

The woman asked what happened to Mrs. Lincoln after she returned to the White House.

She went to bed and stayed there for more than a month, he said. She went to bed in a little spare room she had fixed up for Lincoln's use in the summer, because she refused to enter any of the rooms on the second floor of the White House that were associated with the past, like the bedroom in which her son Willie had lain dying, while his parents gave a party downstairs in the East Room. She felt guilty enough: it was she who had been ambitious, had wanted her husband to be president, had longed to live in this house. She did not attend the funeral. Every blow of the hammers seemed to her like a pistol shot as they built the platform in the East Room for her husband's coffin. She stayed upstairs for six weeks, while people—people off the street, and people on the White House staff—continued stealing the things she had purchased to fix the place up. By the time she left, the china and crystal were already in pawnshops in Georgetown, a Japanese punch bowl she had used as her centerpiece was in a saloon in Baltimore—even the goats Lincoln and her sons had loved had vanished. But when she left, the park ranger said, Mrs. Lincoln was accused of taking it all. She left on May 23, with twenty trunks and fifty boxes. As she departed, the Army of the Potomac was parading past General Grant and President Johnson in front of the White House. She had stayed in the White House almost forty days after Lincoln's murder. She went to Chicago. In Chicago she bought a home but decided she could not afford to live in it, so she moved to a rooming house; and that established the pattern of the remainder of her life, lived out in hotels and pensions, spas and boardinghouses, till she died, seventeen years later, at her sister's, in Springfield, Illinois, in 1882, as homeless as the men sleeping on the benches in the parks of this city. There was a silence when he stopped; then the woman beside me said: "I wonder if she was ever happy again."

Perhaps once on a trip to Scotland with her son Tad, the ranger said; but mostly he didn't think so. Mostly she wandered from place to place. After all, he said, she lost most of her family. She lost one son in infancy, her son Willie in the White House, her son Tad after they returned from Europe. Then her sole surviving child, Robert, thinking

she was mad, had her committed to an insane asylum—
"though it seems," said the ranger, "to have been more like
an insane bed and breakfast, a nice place in the suburbs of
Chicago."

"No place is nice if your son commits you," said the
woman. "What's left of her in Washington that I could see?"

Her dress, he said, on exhibit at the Museum of American History.

"Thank you," she said, and we stepped through the
door. There's a strange thing about Washington: the
quickest way to leave it is to enter the schools of tourist
that are constantly swimming past its monuments and museums. Giving directions to some tired traveler in search of
the White House or Supreme Court, falling in with visitors
from New Hampshire, or Idaho, or Florida, removes you
instantly from the strange mood in which you live in that
city. It was a relief to walk down to the Museum of American History with the woman in the cranberry pants suit
and black fanny pack from Cedar Rapids, Iowa. She had
just driven her daughter to Franklin and Marshall College.
Her husband had died the previous fall of melanoma. In the
Museum of American History we came to a stop in a dark
room before the First Ladies' gowns.

The simplest of them all was a white dress with vertical
black lines, and small embroidered roses: the gown worn in
the portrait taken by Mathew Brady of Mary Lincoln in a
chignon and a headband embroidered with roses, holding

a folded fan, a woman who was not really beautiful but had dressed as if she were, whose faint smile seemed to offer her efforts with a certain hopeful intelligence. The gown, my companion said, had obviously belonged to a woman who loved clothes. That was why her son Robert had had her committed, a docent standing beside us said—her irrational shopping habits. (Indeed, I'd been reading letters to bonnet makers and dressmakers that described the fabrics to be used, the width of borders, the quality of lace, with passionate precision.) By the time she died, the docent said, the bed on which she lay—on one side only, leaving the other for her dead husband—was surrounded by sixty-four trunks with four tons of fabric and clothing inside them (fabric, because the customs duties on cloth were less than those on dresses). A bag lady of sorts, I thought, her life sundered in two the way this city's was—by the war—the nation it presided over before the conflict an agricultural society, an industrial, urban power afterward. After thanking the docent we walked outside onto the Mall. There my companion told me she was driving to Georgia to start the Appalachian Trail; her husband had always wished to do that. I wished her luck.

"Thank you," she said. "I don't know where I'm going, really—I just want to walk."

I wanted to walk too and was grateful for all the things to walk to—the Mall alone having more than one could possibly visit in one day: the National Gallery, the Freer, the Sackler, the Hirshhorn, the National Archives, the Museum of American History, the Museum of Natural History. Then there was, not far away, in the old center of the city, the National Building Museum, where Clinton had held his inaugural ball, and the National Museum of American Art, where Lincoln had held his. The city was a repository of loot, though the more I walked around the more I realized how much was not on display. It was only when I happened to be walking with a historian through Lafayette Square one day that I learned Henry Adams had lived in a town house on the north side, a few doors down from the house he had built near the corner of Sixteenth Street, where the Hay-Adams Hotel now stood, the house designed by H. H. Richardson his wife had never moved into because, just before it was completed, she had gone to her room one morning while her husband sat downstairs reading and swallowed cyanide. In other words, the stories associated with certain blocks in Washington were invisible for the most part, unless you were walking with someone who happened to know that the National Gallery stood on the site of the train station where President Garfield had been assassinated (the second president whose deathbed Robert Lincoln had to sit beside, since he was secretary of war at the time), or the building across the street from the Treasury was where Walt Whitman had worked as a clerk, or the east side of Lafayette Square the home of Mark Hanna, the Ohio boss. There were certainly no plaques, no signs of any of these people or moments in American history. Besides the gown in the Museum of American History there were few traces of Mary Todd Lincoln—or any of the women who'd occupied the Executive Mansion. A pearl necklace, a few of her letters at the Library of Congress, were all that was left; nothing where her husband had been shot (she had never gone to Ford's Theatre again the rest of her life), or in the house where he had died ("this awful place," she'd said). Despite its museums, its monuments, the city of Washington was a vacant shell, a sort of military barracks, or government hall, used by countless people who came and went, like the people who had cut up the curtains in the East Room after Lincoln's murder for souvenirs. Everyone was living in the present. There were concerts and lectures that cost nothing, I noticed in the paper, all over town, cultural events of every conceivable sort. There were so many museums one could spend days on the Mall wandering from one to the next. I did so alone, however; Frank had no interest in museums.

"Museums are morgues!" he said.

Of course, museums are morgues—tombs containing art. Their sepulchral quality was part of their appeal—the dim light, the silence, the tourists wandering through them like ghosts. It was hard to decide which museum resembled a morgue most—the Sackler, which is underground, like a cave in which a Mongol raiding party had hidden its treasure, or the Freer, which felt like the villa of a rich man who has gone abroad and died. The National Archives had the same cold light as the Tomb of Napoleon, and the National Gallery made you feel, when you entered the echoing rotunda, and walked between its dark marble pillars, you were entering the palace of Pluto. They all removed you from the world, though they ejected you back into it at five o'clock, when I would take a slow walk back down the Mall, past the touch football games office staffs played on the Ellipse, darting across the grass with flushed excited faces. "That's what you need to do," said Frank, when I stopped by his apartment one evening before going home. "They're all hanging around the National Gallery, they're tossing a football—like the Kennedys! Find a group and some group activities. It's fun to play a sport after work."

"Then why don't you?" I said.

"Because I don't have the energy. I'm like Sammy," he said, pointing to the battered box by the bed in which his cat traveled with a sign Scotch-taped to the side that read: *Hi! I'm Sammy! I like people! I'm very old and get dehydrated easily, so please give me a drink of water!*

"That describes almost everyone I know," I said as I stood up and turned to look at him.

"But instead of admitting that," said Frank, "like Sammy—that we are dehydrated and need a drink of water—what do people do? Try to appear competent, successful, self-reliant! When in fact we're no better off than this cat! Who, I'm afraid, is about to die." He removed his coat and tie and put on the red silk robe into which he changed the minute he came back from work, to repudiate the long day's struggle at faculty meetings and student conferences and class. "That's my approach," he said, in a slightly altered, heightened voice. "Ask for a drink of water! Because we all need a little drink of water. *A little bit of love!* Meanwhile, give me your coat—that little nylon thing. No one wears down anymore!" he said, taking my bomber jacket when I removed it and holding it out at arm's length. "Take this," he said, going to the closet. "It belonged to my best friend Hans, who died two years ago. I want you to have it. In New York you can wear what you want. In Washington the dress code is stricter—you either look like a homeless drunk or the secretary of state. There's no in-between! And for God's sake, straighten your shoulders. As your mother, I can't overemphasize the importance of posture!"

Walking home with my shoulders back in the big blue overcoat, it felt like my mother had spoken to me—who else cared about your posture? I blended in for the first time: I belonged to Washington. I was one of many men striding down Connecticut Avenue at six o'clock, men with briefcases in topcoats coming home from the office after a long day, or just arriving in cabs at the Mayflower Hotel, the bellhops taking their luggage, while I continued on past the windows of Filene's, filled with wallets, sweaters, and gold watches, and then the Indian restaurant, and finally the outermost edges of Dupont Circle, and then, by a short cut across New Hampshire Avenue, N Street.

My landlord was really one of those men who went out each day in a topcoat and shined shoes and did not come back till evening. He went from his office to his gym after work. The gym, he claimed, was now black—the gay gym had since moved on—and not very friendly; but he had stayed there because the dues were so low. After the gym he often went to dinner with friends; so it was always pitch-dark when he got home. But then he stayed put. There were four bars not half a block from the house, but he never went. One was full of hustlers, he said, who would just as soon slit your throat as look at you; the others reminded him of a life he'd led years ago in which he had no interest now. "I used to stand in Omega for hours," he said, "now I can't even walk in the door. I don't know how people do it." The whole city he seemed to regard that way. Every time I suggested going somewhere he told me I shouldn't even think of going on foot, I would be mugged, I had to take a taxi if I wanted to go at all, that part of town was very dangerous, never forget that Washington was the murder capital of the nation, it was filled with people, he said, who could not control their emotions. When he was home, he was usually on the phone; even when I heard nothing behind the closed doors of his study, however, I was careful to make no noise as I climbed the stairs. And when I reached the stoop, and saw him at the dining room table, going through the mail, if he did not see me, I instinctively turned around and went back down the steps. Sometimes I turned around and went back to the Circle and sat down on a bench.

Once he was in his study, however, with the doors closed, I was able to come and go; and before long I learned his schedule. Each day he left around eight thirty, returned from work or the gym about eight and walked the dog. Then he made up his dinner tray—from the large amounts of chicken parts he boiled en masse and stored in the refrigerator ("This is what happens to my tricks!" he said one evening when he opened the freezer)—went upstairs, watched television, then crossed the landing to his study to return phone calls to people who'd left messages during the day and to work on the ledgers in which he kept track of all the purchases and sales in his store. The voice beyond the study doors—booming, hearty, laughing— depressed me when I heard it. It reminded me that he had friends he saw when he wished to, that there were other people in his life besides me. I spent most of my days alone. That's why it was something of a jolt, and something of a pleasure, when he came home from his day. Around eight o'clock I would be lying on my bed reading the students' work, when I would hear him enter the house downstairs, come up to his study, and greet the dog he had sequestered there all day. "Hey, Biscuit, how ya doin'?" he'd say in a voice both excited and tender. (Often this made me wonder if I should go downstairs to get my greeting too.) Then he took her out for her walk. Then they returned. Then the tray, and TV show. He had his house, he had his friends, his *Will & Grace*—and that was it. At fifty-five things had stopped happening to him, I suspected. Nothing happened to him anymore. Or rather: Everything that did had already happened before—many, many times.

In other words, my landlord, like most of us, had accumulated a set of habits—routines that were the substance of his day, a daily rosary that ended when he made sure the double doors to his study were closed and he sat down at his desk to balance his accounts—working for himself and not the government. Going over these numbers must have pleased him in some elemental way. He reminded me of an older America that had never changed its values of thrift, cleanliness, and order; the only difference was that he was homosexual, and therefore had led a life different from the one expected of him. The homosexual part, however, was now inactive. He was now a sort of homosexual emeritus. Sex had left him in its wake. He was a man who'd been riding the rapids of a river, who finally finds a cove, a still pool, and pauses there to catch his breath—though after a while he realizes it's not just a pause, but rather the place he has ended up, beached in the sunlight, exhausted, no longer able to get in that cold and tumultuous river again.

One Saturday I was eating lunch downstairs thinking of the meals my mother was fed when she could not have felt the slightest appetite when I glanced out the window and saw him in the street trying to unload a chest of drawers from his van. I rushed outside to help. "No, no, you don't really have to, I'm okay," he said; and then, moments later, grunting and gasping as we struggled up the stairs with an armoire: "This is really nice of you." The landing, I saw, was already crowded with furniture he'd hauled up— chairs, lamps, candelabra, paintings he'd just bought, he said, at an estate sale on New Hampshire Avenue. "Every Saturday you find treasures," he said in a voice of childlike wonder as we paused on the landing to catch our breath. "There are yard sales all over Northwest, *objets* somebody decided no longer express his current mood! Gay men are so fickle!" he said with a laugh. "They change their décor more often than their gym! You know, I really appreciate this," he said. "I really do."

"It's nothing," I said as we went back for another chest.

The next day, on the stairs, I found an envelope with my name on it, and a formal card inside thanking me in the most polite way for my help.

But there was nothing else I could do to help, it seemed, as I lay upstairs reading through the long still mornings before I had to go to school, listening to the occasional call trigger my landlord's hearty voice on his answering machine. I was in that house a lot, my duties at school were so light. Tuesdays I taught class, Thursdays I held office hours (nobody came), Saturdays I sometimes went to school to use the copying machine when nobody else was there or to simply give my landlord the impression I had something to do. But much of my time I had no real reason to leave the house. My landlord, on the other hand, was out every day. He had a full and busy life, which he seemed to have organized with admirable efficiency. The only element that seemed to have been left out of the equation was his dog. His dog spent the long mornings and afternoons alone, in the study behind closed doors. One day, on an impulse, returning to my room after lunch, I opened the doors, and poked my head in to see how she was. She was lying on a discolored piece of carpet, curled up behind a chair against the wall—so used to being there she merely raised her head to regard me with her sad dark eyes, then lowered her face onto her paws again with a mournful expression, resuming a pose of infinite resignation. Not wishing to interfere, I withdrew from the room and closed the doors. She was not mine, after all—I'd been taking care of someone who had been, but this dog was my landlord's. Still I wondered how the dog could lie there all day—how she passed the hours—what concept of time, if any, she had, whether being left alone depressed her, or whether to a dog all things were simply phenomena the dog did not judge, things with no context, no past or future. The next day in the middle of another silent afternoon, while reading on my bed, I thought of her again—went down, opened the doors, and this time left them open. Walking back upstairs I waited for her to follow but she did not. Then when I returned to close the doors the dog did not even lift her head to watch.

The dog, it occurred to me one day, was not unlike Mrs. Lincoln, stuck in the back on the top floor of a hotel, where the rooms were cheaper. Perhaps it was this letter of Mrs. Lincoln's ("*I do want* a quiet, home & *there* to remain & wander no more . . . It mortifies me, in *this* land, for which my beloved husband's precious life was sacrificed, that I am unable, in my gloom, to shelter myself under my own roof—.") that made me think of the dog that had been left behind, was all alone, had too much empty time to fill on these winter afternoons. *Surely the dog will make the connection*, I thought, *between the open doors and freedom*. But she did not. She stayed where she was, on her piece of shag carpet turned yellow with age and use.

Each time I went to visit her, however, I stayed longer in the study to look around. The study had two tall windows, bookcases, club chairs, a beautiful cherrywood desk, and a table on which a small plastic radio was playing music at a very low volume, to keep the dog company, I assumed, like the television that nursing home aides leave on in the room of a patient who is otherwise ignored. The study was a cave of books—histories, travel guides, murder mysteries, novels. The histories were mostly American—Henry Adams, Grant's memoirs, biographies of Lincoln, *The Day Kennedy Was Shot*. One wall was covered with framed photographs: people shaking my landlord's hand, my landlord on hikes and picnics, my landlord at a Mayan temple in a jungle, on an island above a turquoise sea. *A full American life*, I thought, *travel included*. On his desk were photographs of family members. One shelf of the bookcase contained nothing but scrapbooks—pictures of my landlord at a gay pride march, the beach, a piazza in Rome. One day while perusing my landlord's youth I noticed the dog had stood up. Slowly she advanced to my feet, where she stopped and looked up at me, as if to ask what I meant. Then she went back to her little piece of ratty yellowed carpet and lay down.

The next day she got up when I entered the study as if she'd been waiting for me; then followed me out to the landing and finally down the stairs. On the landing she paused to look down at a house she seldom saw at this time of day. Then she proceeded to descend the stairs in halting, careful stages, stopping to look down at what awaited her, resuming a normal posture only when her toenails finally began clicking on the golden wood of the ground floor, as if the sound had convinced her this was real.

That day and every one after I gave her the run of the house—though when I opened the doors to the garden, thinking this would give her the most freedom, she surprised me by stopping at the door and staring outside—as if that she could not even comprehend. She had no interest in going out. She turned round and went back into the living room. What she seemed to like most was what I enjoyed too: sitting on the spine of the sofa downstairs watching people go by on the street.

There was always someone going by, but no matter what it was she never barked. She was a silent dog—a small, fine-boned, intelligent-looking animal bred in Africa, my landlord said, to catch rats. She seemed as mesmerized by the people passing the house as I was, including the battered, weathered man in the plaid jacket who picked up fallen leaves one by one and placed them in his pocket—the Vietnam veteran the block had hired to keep it neat who was, my landlord said, "not quite all there." He never once glanced up at the house. When we were not seated on the sofa watching the street, the dog and I played a game I triggered accidentally one day by bending down in front of her. The instant I did this she bent down, too, lowered her chest to the floor, and extended her paws, so that her haunches rose, just like the pose in yoga called Downward Facing Dog—and then, when I backed up, she started twirling in circles, like a dervish. Then finally she barked and ran after me. Then, after letting off steam, we would return to the sofa by the front window, where she'd perch on top of it on her stomach, as still and fine as an Egyptian statuette, watching the street till it grew dark, which meant my landlord would be coming home—at which point I took her back upstairs, returned her to the dark study, and closed the doors.

Across the hall I learned what my landlord had been reading before he went to sleep. Sometimes it was a serious book—on global population problems, the proliferation of nuclear weapons, the problems of the Middle East—other times, just a murder mystery. It was strange that the bedroom doors were never closed during the day: the room most people keep private. The décor, which had seemed so cutting-edge in the seventies (chrome and glass, gray walls and carpet), now looked, incredibly (since we always imagine our era's taste to be classic), dated. The dark gray comforter that covered the low bed pulled up neatly to the gray cross-grained pillowcases, the cubelike table beside the bed under the retractable reading lamp with the book on it, were extremely neat, almost ascetic; on the other side of the room was something more hedonistic: a hot tub with mirrored walls and a cluster of bottles with silver caps, a vase with a single gladiola (the seventies flower), and on the wall some silver-framed photographs of building cornices with sunlight falling across them in different patterns.

All of this had been chic thirty years ago but was now just that: the seventies. Still it must have represented his idea of urban refinement. "What are the people where you grew up like?" I asked him one evening as we were preparing our dinners.

"Mean and stupid!" he said.

His town, he explained, had a Baptist college from which he'd graduated before coming to Washington as an intern;

everyone there was homophobic. Like a lot of gay men, he said, he'd come to D.C. for the same reason the slaves had after the Civil War. "The federal government!" he said. When he was an intern he had worked in an office that looked right down into the offices of another building just like his, where he could see men sitting at their desks reading the paper. One day he asked his boss what they were doing, and his boss said, "Drawing salaries." He told his boss that's just what he wanted to do. At the time he had an office with no windows. Next he asked how you got an office with a window, and his boss said, "You go to law school." So he went to law school. "And now I draw a salary in an office with a window—just like the men I used to see," he said. "You can't imagine how stupid it all is. But they can't fire me. The whole government, you know, is run by gays and Jews." He seemed to make light of everything he did—till when I pressed him, he admitted he worked for the Department of Labor on regulations pertaining to safety in coal mines.

But though he had successfully escaped the small town where everyone was mean and stupid by becoming a government attorney, there was still something about his past he could not shake, apparently, because he was still so sensitive to denunciations of homosexuality. Even the neighbors here concerned him. When a house on the block changed hands, he seemed relieved that a flight attendant and his attorney-lover had bought the place, as if he was worried that the neighborhood was becoming too hetero-sexual. The rest of the world was even more threatening. He always left *The Washington Post* for me on the dining room table—he was so neat that even though he'd read it, it looked new, though sometimes a story in the paper so up-set him he ripped it out and wrote an apology to me in the margin. Then when he came home he would tell me that it was about Jerry Falwell or Pat Robertson. My landlord was, so far as I could tell, like many gay men of a certain age, celibate—because of AIDS, or an inability to attract the partners they wanted, or simply diminishing interest. But he was still angry about the milieu in which he had grown up. Despite his job, his life in the city, his house, there was still something anxious about him—like a man who's entered a witness protection program but thinks even in his new town he may be assassinated. He no longer had sex, but he got all the more angry when anyone chal-lenged his right to do so. One evening he paused on the landing, turned to me, and said: "Did you see what Falwell said in today's paper, that fat pig? He said we're all going to burn in Hell. His daughter has gay friends, I know some of them. But he's still saying that we're going to burn in Hell."

He did not look like someone who would burn in Hell, whatever that look is; like so many men in Northwest Washington, he exuded middle-class propriety. When he set out in the morning in his black overcoat, with cell

· *47* ·

phone, briefcase, and umbrella, he was one of legions of men who worked in the big faceless office buildings downtown. On the weekends he wore khaki pants and faded flannel shirts that concealed his swelling gut—his efforts at the gym defeated by his habit of eating peanut butter straight from the jar. He loved the arts. He was often out at some cultural event. He had a subscription to the Kennedy Center and two repertory groups; though most of the theater he saw disappointed, and a production of a play about South Africa (Athol Fugard's *The Island*), the night I was sitting in the dining room when he got home, could still plunge him into shock.

"It was unbelievable," he said in a tone of wonderment as he paused on his way upstairs, "the worst thing I've ever seen. But the audience—all white, of course—gave it a standing ovation."

The theater—like homosexuality—was apparently something he still wanted to believe in but which no longer rewarded his original passion; nevertheless, like the Lincolns, he went to at least a play a week. He'd wanted, in fact, to be a stage designer but had thought better of it, he said, his senior year. Now the only set he worked on was his house. I would come downstairs to find he'd used the furniture from a yard sale to transform the living room into a porch in the South Seas—all white wicker—or something Belle Epoque. One morning I walked onto the landing to find a shimmering bolt of blue cloth suspended from the skylight outside my room to the floor two stories below. In the same spirit he lighted his house every night for the benefit of passersby, that anonymous audience that would glance in on a winter evening to see a single spotlight burnishing the *Boy with a Thorn*, or a softer light on the rococo mirror, or a vase of tulips on the dining room table under a pin light. Some nights he sat downstairs on the small sofa, stroking the dog in his lap, and watched people go by, like a playwright watching his audience. Other nights he would bolt when he saw me coming up the stairs outside, and by the time I entered the house, the parlor would be empty. One night he was perched on the sofa laughing when I entered the house. "You won't believe what just happened," he said. "I was sitting here looking out the window, when four gorgeous guys in full leather came to a stop on the sidewalk and began staring up at me—absolutely staring. I couldn't believe it. Then, just as I was about to invite them, Biscuit wagged her tail and I realized it wasn't me they were looking at, it was my dog! It's not easy being an aging actress," he laughed.

"It's not easy being alive," said Frank to me the next day as we sat down in Dupont Circle. "Let's face it—like the rest of us, your landlord has no idea, I'm sure, why he's still here—what the others were doing that he was not. That's your landlord's problem, you know."

"What?"

"He's one of thousands of gay men who survived AIDS

only to realize they are completely alone and have nothing to live for," he said.

"I asked him the other day how many friends he'd lost to AIDS," I said, "and do you know what he said?"

"What?"

"Three to six hundred. That must be an exaggeration."

"Not in his case," he said. "You don't know what D.C. was like during the eighties. Funerals, funerals, funerals! I got my suntan one summer from just standing in Rock Creek Cemetery. It was a nightmare. I used to think the eighties were like a very nice dinner party with friends, except some of them were taken out and shot while the rest of us were expected to go on eating."

"But then the whole city must remind you of people who aren't here."

"But that's why *you* should live here—you have no memories. You have no past. Here."

He stood up.

"So he did lose a lot of friends."

"Of course," he said.

"But then why is he . . . so cheerful?"

"Cheerful! Cheerful? He's polite!" He lighted a cigarette. "I'm afraid you may be misinterpreting our mutual friend in the light of your own rather desperate wants and needs! What's it like over there, anyway, when you're both home?" he said.

"We live very quietly, like two old bachelors. That's what's so nice. He works in his study balancing his books and I lie upstairs reading the letters of Mrs. Lincoln."

"Not still," he said. "You know, you really have to ask yourself why you're obsessing on this woman."

"Do you know what was written on the inside of her wedding ring?"

"What?"

"*Love Is Eternal*," I said.

"Ah," said Frank. "That's nice. I wonder if I could get the Lug to give me one of those. He wants us to get married, you know."

"Utter devotion to one person," I said.

"Me," he said.

"That's right," I said.

"But that still leaves you. Have you tried speed dating? That thing where they put you in a room with forty other men and you all have three minutes to ask each other questions? Of course that entails a great risk—that no one will want to date you. That's *your* problem, you know."

"What?" I said.

"You want to be needed! But your landlord's not in a nursing home. However, you could help *me* put on my cold cream," he said in an altered voice. "Or sit with me a while until I fall asleep."

"Stop it," I said.

"Is that a no?" he said, retaining the voice. "I'm not surprised. You probably have more important things to do at your age. I just thought maybe you might like to help. I thought perhaps you might even, dare I say, care for me. But I can see that this was an illusion. Oh, look," he said, as someone our age walked into the Circle in tight blue jeans and a baseball cap. "Another case of age-inappropriate fashion! That's one mistake your landlord doesn't make, like these bozos, who make you think it really is all just a case of arrested development," he said as the man our age went by, "as if they still see themselves as twenty-five. No, your landlord dresses very well. He doesn't try to play a role he's far too old for."

The role he played in my opinion came to me quite accidentally one day in the Freer Gallery when I came upon a Chinese scroll painting of a lake hemmed in by steep and snowy mountains, and a little house that contained, when I looked closely, two figures. *On a gloomy winter afternoon,* the text beside the painting said, *a scholar sits in his elegant pavilion as a kneeling servant prepares some warm tea.* That's my landlord, I thought—especially when he closed the doors of his study each evening after work. He seemed to have everything one could want but one—a companion— and the problem there, he said when we were discussing the general issue one day, was that men his age were not attracted to one another. "They're all looking for someone younger," he said. "Just like straight men." So my landlord lived alone, except for his tenant, in a house as still and silent as a pavilion in a winter landscape on a Chinese scroll.

"He *is* his house," was my explanation one day when Frank stopped by to visit, as we sat downstairs waiting for my landlord to put the dog on a leash upstairs so that we could all go to Dupont Circle together. "Look around you," I said. He did, commenting on this and that, till my landlord came down with Biscuit. Though he pulled vigorously at the leash, keeping her close to him, the minute we sat down on a bench in the Circle, she began keening at the sight of another dog passing through the park. "She never does that," my landlord said. The sustained sound was not a bark but something so full of longing and frustrated desire it seemed cruel that she could not pursue her desire for this other dog because she was on a leash, a leash kept firmly in hand by a man no more free to pursue what he wanted than she was, I could not help thinking, though he did not emit a keening sound deep in his throat, he simply said: "I want that," when someone his type (stocky, muscular, broad-chested, dark-haired, about thirty) walked by.

"That's where I interview the people who reply to my ad in the Personals," my landlord said, nodding at the hotel on Nineteenth Street. "A nice, impersonal lobby you can always get out of quickly if you have to."

"I've used that lobby myself," Frank said, "for the same reason. Only I wasn't interviewing *them*—they were interviewing *me*. And if I was lucky, I got a nice cocktail before we went upstairs, if you get my drift."

Just then a group of young men walked past our bench. "Wouldn't you think they could just look once?" my landlord said. "What is it—do I have shit on my head?"

"No," said Frank, "but if you had a smart little cloche from Lily Dache, I think that might get their attention."

My landlord laughed. "There are a lot of good-looking men in this town," he said, "many of whom get whiplash when they see me coming down the street, they look away so fast. Like the guys at this party I went to last night— A-list Washington! Each guy more gorgeous than the last. Some of them would actually talk to you—though the minute you start chatting, you can hear them turn the meter on. They'll give you just so many seconds, so you won't think them stuck up, and then the taxi ride is over!"

"On paper he's perfect," I told Frank, as we watched my landlord wend his way home through the traffic. (He never stayed long; it was as if there were some urgent business calling him away, though what that could be I could not imagine.) "He's attractive, appropriately dressed, owns his own house, mostly paid for, with several rental properties besides, a good job, and says he wants a partner. But he's alone! What's wrong with this picture?"

"You tell me," Frank said.

"Well, I can only judge by my own experience," I said, "but I suspect casual sex is beyond him now. Because there's nothing casual about sex to a man who's looking at the problem of long-term nursing home insurance. Who's wondering who will drive him to the hospital when he has to go—who, when he looks up on those quiet evenings at home and wonders, why he *is* alone, hears a voice say: 'Because we spent our lives having the sort of sex that was accompanied by an unwritten guarantee that it was completely dissociated from any form of emotional or social attachment whatsoever.' I mean how many of us were ever really able to integrate sex with the rest of our lives? And now we realize we're not looking for sex anymore—we're looking for fidelity. Tenderness! Intimacy! And that's why he's going to put an ad in the Personals."

"WHEN I DID this ten years ago," my landlord said, looking up from the tablet on which he was composing the ad when I got home, "I was forty-five, and I got almost a hundred responses. Two years ago, at fifty-three, I got eight. So this time I should get . . . two." He smiled. "But I'm going to do it anyway—and see who the lucky pair will be!"

Instead of responses from the lucky pair, I placed nothing but postcards for the next few weeks on the hall table, which friends had sent from Sydney and Bangkok, Taormina and Rio de Janeiro, with veiled references (suitable for the postmistress's eyes) to the sex they were having with the natives; my landlord scooped them up from the hall table when he came home, put them on his dinner tray, and went upstairs to a solitary supper. The homosexual emeritus was just that: though placing a personal ad in the paper seemed on the surface to imply he had hopes, placing it in a newspaper (the seventies venue) seemed like more of a gesture for its own sake, since most people these days were using the computer.

At night, on the computer, the subterranean lust, the frustration, the resentment of lonely men erupted in postings on Web sites that read like letters to Miss Lonelyhearts, or, more accurately, obscene graffiti—demands so pornographic they could never be met in this world (which may have been the point). Real life was more difficult. One afternoon, when I was leaving the National Gallery, a bearded man coming up the steps with a camera slung across his shoulder fixed his eyes on mine—a glance so longed for, it plunged me into a kind of anger, so that by the time I got home, and blurted out what had just happened to my landlord, it sounded more like a mugging. But he understood exactly. "What were you supposed to do?" he said. "Stop and turn around and say: 'Are you in a hotel?' I don't think so! Do you suppose anyone still does that anymore? As if the past had never happened. As if everyone weren't dead!"

He was fed up with bars, with meat markets, he told me, and people who were still going to sex clubs, and a lot of other things: the rudeness of the cashiers at CVS, the masseur he'd stopped going to because he told my landlord the penis size of his other customers, the futility of May-December romances, the delusion of Caucasians looking for Asian boyfriends twenty years younger than themselves, the conformity and status-snobbery of gay men in Washington, where, at every party you went to, everyone was wearing the same sweater and the same shoes, and all of them looking for someone who did not exist. He said he got angry when people didn't cruise him, and furious when they did. "Everyone's depressed," he said one night. "Every day I find out another friend is on Paxil or Wel-butrin. It's like *The Invasion of the Body Snatchers*! What kind of a country have we made?" Then an hour later he knocked gently on the wall beside my open door and said, "Sorry to bother you—but there's a Quaker meeting up the block tomorrow night at six thirty that is supposedly a very good place to meet people. Would you like to go? I'll stop by after work and get you."

"Oh, not the Quaker meeting!" Frank said when I told him on the phone where we were going. "The Quaker meeting is the last resort—the place you go when every other attempt fails—the graveyard of hope, the foul rag-and-bone shop of the heart! But go, maybe you'll meet someone!"

"FLY, FLY LIKE the wind!" my landlord said as we dashed through the cars circling Dupont Circle the next evening.

Yet when we reached the opposite sidewalk he came to a stop and said, "There's really no need to hurry. There's probably no reason to go to this. If it hasn't worked by now, it's not likely to—I mean after years and years of this you really have to conclude: Something about this is just not working! We're beating our heads against a wall. But this place used to be very good if you were looking."

This place turned out to be a Georgian house on Florida Avenue; upon entering an usher took us to a small waiting room in which other people sat staring down at their shoes like people on a subway, until the usher came and led us to a dark wooden door that opened into a large, high-ceilinged room with Palladian windows looking out onto a garden bordered with rhododendron bushes. There was no cross, no pulpit—no singing, incense, or ceremony. The people sat quietly, waiting, like satellite dishes, for the Holy Ghost to inspire them as they listened to the rain drip on the rhododendrons. They were gathered in a room—like people at a sickbed—to wait for God to inspire them to speak; like Mary Lincoln holding séances in the White House after the loss of her son Willie, and later after she'd left the White House and lost her husband. Finally a man stood up, and then a woman, and then another man. What they said was like Washington itself: polite, idealistic, and cerebral. "That one's so hot," my landlord whispered as he nodded at a man two pews away from us. "His lover died two years ago and left him a lot of money, which he spent on travel and drugs. Then he got sick, and looked really awful, but the cocktail brought him back, and now he's gorgeous again!

"Well, how are you?" said my landlord to a couple of men holding the hands of a small child between them as we walked out. "How's it goin'?"

"Not getting much sleep," one said.

"But it's worth it," said the other.

"Well, that's great," said my landlord. "That's really great! Good luck!" Then he lowered his voice as they went around the corner and said, "They say the kids from Russia are not all there mentally. Do you think that's where it ends up—adopting? I find the whole thing freaky."

Each time we stopped to talk to people he knew I was introduced with the explanation that I would be living with him till April 20—a date my landlord seemed to have memorized, like the combination to his lock at the gym, or the date his mortgage was due. And each time he did so I felt rebuked; as if any illusions I had about our sharing the house were just that—I was there for a limited and very definite term. "You know so many people!" I said as we walked back to the house.

"I used to know a lot more," he said, brushing his moustache with his fingertips. "But even now, I can't keep up. In a city like this everyone just floats around thinking *somebody* they meet will bring them love or success or a connection. Well, sport," he said when we reached the corner,

"I don't know about you, but I'm heading home. I've got a long day tomorrow researching an amendment on the diameter of the wheels and axle size of the trucks mining supervisors are allowed to use underground when making their inspection rounds. Really important stuff," he said, glancing across the street at the people in Dupont Circle. For a moment I hoped he would suggest we sit there—but he decided to deny himself this pleasure, and since there seemed no point in doing it alone, I told him I'd go home too. In fact I would have done whatever he wanted to do. The very fact of returning with him to the house produced a feeling of intimacy—even if, once there, we went to our separate floors. Lying upstairs in that house, we were like spiders on the same web; I was aware of the slightest nuance of the stillness in the air between us. It was a pleasure to read in that quiet house knowing he was on the floor beneath. The first month, when he had left for the weekend, I had luxuriated in my solitude; now, when he was gone, the house felt lonely. Even when he was home, however, I made myself leave. I was here to start life over, and to start life over you had to go out.

Just before leaving, after putting on my overcoat, I would look at myself in the mirror downstairs—and sometimes go back upstairs because of what I saw in it. Yet I had to do this before I could exit the house—as if, like the mirror in a fairy tale, everything else was false, and only its reflection true. *You poor thing*, I would think, then go back to my room, take off the coat, and lie down; or lie down with my clothes still on and think of what I might be doing had I not come here at all. I would be home in my own house, I would think, as safe as the dog in the study, where no one could see me, and there was no need to look in a mirror before going out, because there would be no one on the street outside when I did, especially since back home I waited till after dark to walk. That was one reason I had moved here—because I was waiting till dark to leave the house in that little town—though here too I waited for night; because at night I could not be seen.

When my landlord was home in the evening, there was no need to leave. What is better than reading in the same room or same house with someone at night? Reading is an activity both communal and separate. The lighted lamps, the quiet, the knowledge that my landlord was downstairs, all made me happy: the two of us seemed to constitute a household then; that home for which everyone is looking. In truth, of course, I felt my status as a boarder all the more keenly at such moments.

It was this feeling that sometimes made me dress and go out for a walk even on nights when my landlord was home; though even then, before I left, I had to know what he was doing. Whether the study doors were closed or not when I slipped downstairs, whether he was talking on the telephone and laughing, or across the landing in his bedroom, with its doors closed, watching television or reading, had to be ascertained. Downstairs I interpreted even the lights he had chosen to leave on. The lights were a form of communication, too. I parsed them for clues to the nature of our relationship. When I got home from my walk at night, for instance, the house was always lighted, since he had no idea if I had returned when he went to bed; and I, not knowing if he was out, would leave the lights on when I went up to my room. The possibility that one of us was still out meant neither one of us extinguished the lights, which sometimes burned till morning—suggesting a nocturnal social life neither person had anymore.

These little courtesies deepened the feeling of intimacy. Yet when I lay upstairs, half-reading and half-looking at the room, so pleasantly lighted, a certain anxiety always spoiled the pleasure I felt in being in that comfortable house—because it was his house, not mine. Even my landlord suggested I buy a place—as if he wanted me to settle in Washington—where everyone eventually talked about real estate, and the great division between people seemed to be between those who owned and those who rented.

Mary Lincoln, I now knew, had bought a house in Chicago not long after the assassination and lived there for a while—but the executor of Lincoln's will withheld the funds due her from the estate to the point that she believed herself unable to continue paying the mortgage; so she moved out and rented the house. What murder was to Lady Macbeth shopping was to Mary Lincoln, it seemed;

shopping, and its flip side—the fear of being poor. On that she was irrational. "It is difficult," her son Robert said, after he'd had her committed, "dealing with someone who is sane in every respect but one"—though I could not decide if it was her paranoia about being poor, or something deeper (her sense that there was no point in having a home, without her husband) that had led her to give up the house on West Washington Street so soon after buying it. Then came the debacle of trying to raise money by selling her dresses and jewels in New York; and her escape and long traipse through Europe—a journey whose hopelessness I thought of when Frank took me around to look at apartment buildings one morning. The curious thing about Washington is that a city set apart for the whole nation cannot be claimed by any single citizen—many of whom regard it as their home nevertheless. Frank, in fact, seemed to know the floor plans of half of the apartment buildings we passed; not to mention the people who lived in them, and what place they occupied in the detailed honeycomb of status-conscious Washington. "Notice, for instance, how she's dressed," he said as a gray-haired woman in dark glasses and a silver scarf turned into a building on Scott Circle. "It's such an indication of what's inside. I can almost tell you what a one bedroom will look like by how the woman who lives there drapes her scarf. I could take you up Connecticut Avenue right now and show you women living alone at every conceivable level of hygiene and taste! My mother lived on Connecticut Avenue, in the sixties, after my father died—I had to go there and play bridge with her every Wednesday and Saturday night. She wanted me to move in with her, but I refused. I wanted to live in the Miramar. That's Spanish, you know, for 'view of the sea'—though there is no sea. That's Washington," he said, looking, in his own dark glasses and shock of blond hair, too glamorous for his native city. "My mother would never have lived in the Miramar," he said, coming to a stop before a big brick building on Fifteenth Street. "But it might be just what you are looking for—a room with a hot plate, a place for tricks!"

The Miramar had a waiting list, we learned upon inquiring inside, and an application form one had to fill out, which Frank helped me with, till we got to a space for "Project or Purpose in Washington." The two of us paused. Then Frank said, turning to me: "Why don't you write 'Aging homosexual seeks to reinvent life'?"

Instead we left that space blank and handed the form to the woman at the desk. Then I went back to the house on N Street. I was eager to return to my laptop to see if there was a message from the African-American dentist I'd met in a chat room. He was very definite about what he wanted to do; I had only to come over. But it was always late when we talked, and I said it would be better to wait till the next day.

One reason I never went was just that my landlord was downstairs—his solitude seemed to approve my own. We were a family now: he and I and the dog. I especially liked it when the dog appeared in my doorway, having wandered upstairs, out of curiosity or boredom; she seemed to me an envoy—sent to see how I was doing.

One morning at breakfast I found the nerve to ask why he kept the dog shut up in the study all day while he was gone. "Because when I don't," he said, "she gets up on the furniture and ruins my chairs with those big *rat-catching* toenails of hers." On the one hand, I thought, he was being realistic, and that was that; on the other, the dog's incarceration seemed a high price to pay for the well-being of one's furniture. "He runs a tight ship," Frank said one evening as we sat in Dupont Circle. "Some people are good at that. Some people make a home for themselves. Others," he said, looking around at the men sprawled on the benches around us, "are doomed to float down the River of Life, like limbs that have broken off the trees—flotsam and jetsam, if you get my drift."

They both wanted me to buy an apartment; though I only pretended to be looking. In truth I was just walking. Some nights, just the sound of my landlord's contented laughter in the study drove me from the house, even though I had to manufacture some objective, like the White House, for the stroll. The emptiness of Lafayette

Square at night was always soothing. That was the pleasure of the city after dark: it was empty. Most people were home. Often, when I was walking back from the Mall, the bell of the Episcopal church began to ring as I was crossing the square, and I would feel myself in another century—when church bells had been more common—and try to imagine Henry Adams reading in his library on the north side of the square, convinced the United States would collapse in the year 1951—and the whole effrontery of building a house across from the White House became clear.

But there was no way to imagine his grief, standing there by the Hay-Adams Hotel, any more than you can communicate with the dead by standing in a cemetery. Most of the time I was just taking a walk. Certain routes, by the time I'd been there a couple of months, had become so routine that I no longer even noticed anything on the way. Eventually I crossed Lafayette Square so many times I ceased to think of Adams or the fact that Seward lived on the east side of the park when he was nearly killed the night Lincoln was shot. What continued to soothe me was the emptiness of the city after dark. It was the perfect city for grief: like walking through a cemetery. At night the National Gallery looked like an enormous mausoleum: like that temple the boaters are headed toward in Böcklin's *Isle of the Dead*. On each side of its huge brass doors a torchère cast a strange light on the smooth stone—that colorless light one wants to call, but isn't, yellow or green that you find in the National Archives; the kind of light which is used so that the objects it falls upon will not decompose—the light that preserves documents, and suggests the Underworld. There was no one to see it. But it looked like the temple of some ancient city on the eve of battle—a city near which thousands of soldiers lay sleeping; though in reality, the only person nearby was the occasional lone Marine jogging down the gravel path, wide-eyed and sweating in the dark. Then one evening on the Mall the sound of my own footsteps made me come to a stop. It was not physical fatigue. It was the sound of those footsteps—and the fact that these walks were going nowhere. It seemed to me at that moment that if I sat down on the curb I would never move again. I was all alone—the Capitol blazing white in the night, the scalloped roofs of the Smithsonian Castle visible against a dirty gray sky. Physical energy is not the only thing that enables you to take a walk; the spirit must be willing, too. When I finally made it back to the house, I found the dog lying beside my landlord on his bed, the only creature that meant anything to me now, even though she looked at me through the open bedroom doors as if I meant nothing to her at all as I passed on my way upstairs.

The next morning I went into the study and freed the dog and then went back up to my room, where the dog soon followed, and lay down beside me as I read. It was so quiet in the house I put down my book to listen to the silence, and watched the pigeons roosting on a high brick wall behind the house, and, beyond that, a crane moving building materials from the ground to the tenth story of the steel skeleton of yet another hotel going up on the opposite block. Then, after watching the ivy turn over onto its light green side in the wind, I opened the book again and read another letter from the woman who believed that any attempt to be happy was beside the point, since she was only waiting to be reunited with her husband and children in the afterlife.

In the way that books can take over your life, the letters of Mrs. Lincoln were starting to be the reference for everything I noticed. She was now in a hotel in Frankfurt. ("All the nobility stop here, counts, dukes & dutchesses abound in the house, and on my table, their cards are frequently laid. Yet in consideration of poor health & deep mourning, I have of course accepted no dinner invitations & have kept very quiet. Popp, the most charming of *all* dress makers, who receives many orders from America, and makes for the royal family of Prussia & all the nobility, has just made me up some heavy mourning silks, richly trimmed with crape. The *heaviest* blk English Crape here, is only in our money $1.50 cts per yard, think of it! when in *war* times—I once gave, *ten* dollars per yard, for the *heaviest*!") She seemed excited at first to be there. ("I like Frankfurt exceedingly, the true secret is, I suppose I am enjoying peace, which in my deepest, heart rending sorrow, I was not allowed, in my native land!") But the note of anguish soon entered in. ("I find it quite as expensive here as in America & as I am urged by my physicians to proceed to Italy very soon—at least I expect to start about the 22d of January & remain until 1st April. *That* fearful, sorrowful month, will be spent very quietly here on my return.") Finally the relief at having escaped the American newspapers' criticism of her attempt to sell her clothes, her excitement at being in Europe, among aristocrats and superior couturiers, were spoiled by the demons she had brought with her: her fear that she could not afford the hotel or avoid people's stares, her inconsolable grief, in which, dressed as she was (for the rest of her life) in mourning, it seemed she was trapped. The longer she remained in Frankfurt, the higher up, the further back, the smaller, the cheaper, the room was, till by the time her friend Mrs. Orne—a wealthy woman from Philadelphia who tried hard to get Mrs. Lincoln a pension from Congress—found her, she was living in what seemed to be a garret.

There was a room across the hall from mine that reminded me of the room in which Mrs. Orne had found her friend, and they had spent three days together, weeping and carrying on so loudly a guest down the hall knocked on the door to ask them to shut up. My landlord's spare room was used for storage—things he bought for his store in the mountains: a collection that ran the gamut from feathered headdresses to mannequins to pieces of heavy furniture. Every now and then he would come up the stairs to survey its contents; one day he showed me a chest of drawers that had been owned by the daughter of Grover Cleveland, a woman, he said, who had died in a local nursing home. As we were standing in that room, with its cramped ceiling, looking down into the street below, it was easy to imagine the Frankfurt hotel room—the sort of room Mrs. Lincoln would eventually end up in wherever she stayed because it was cheaper than the rest, and, no doubt, more hidden. Some evenings I'd come home and find my landlord at the dining room table, still in his jacket and tie, reading the newspaper as he waited for his plate of chicken parts to thaw, and think of the dining room in the hotel where Mrs. Lincoln ate alone, ignoring the stares of the other guests, the whispers of "Mrs. Lincoln, Mrs. Lincoln, Mrs. Lincoln." Like the tone of her letters from Europe, my landlord's moods seemed to veer between impulses of exhibitionism ("I must throw a party while you're here") and a desire for seclusion. What surprised me was how many evenings he spent alone. After his theater subscription was done he hardly left the house. When, after pausing on my way upstairs one night to say I was thinking of walking to a certain bar, I asked if he wanted to come with me, he looked up, and said: "God, no! It's all pimps and prostitutes. A guy was murdered there last year. Plus there's a new outbreak of syphilis, you know—it was in the paper. Thanks, but I'm in for the night." And I thought of her on the top floor of the hotel in a room at the back, where she finally found it easier to have her meals alone, as my landlord finished with: "Remember, it's not our town, it's theirs!"

I wasn't sure if he was referring to the racial apartheid he'd mentioned the night we'd met, or the snobbery of the young, who walked by him as if he were a ghost; but my landlord was quite as apprehensive about the world as Mrs. Lincoln. He told me not to go near Logan Circle, so recently a red-light district, or down to the Eagle or the baths—gay men were bashed and murdered near these places—though when I mentioned this to Frank one evening, Frank said: "Oh, that's nonsense. Things were bad over there when Marion Barry was in office, but now it's perfectly fine. In fact, it's what this neighborhood used to be in the seventies, when people started fixing up the houses here. If I were a twenty-three-year-old gay man who'd just moved to Washington, that's just where I'd want to live." The only reason my landlord went there one day with Frank and me was to see the Whole Foods that had opened just west of Fourteenth Street.

Logan Circle was indeed now what my landlord's neighborhood had been years before: a place gay men had rescued from decrepitude. That too was part of my landlord's isolation, I assumed—the strange way he seemed to have retired from life already. The locus of gay life was moving eastward, leaving my landlord and his house relics of the past. These streets had come full circle: the place where millionaires built mansions in the 1800s that displayed their wealth was now, after decades of destitution, looking once more like a section of Boston's Back Bay at the turn of the century—a curve of mansions and town houses round a park. There was nothing more agreeable in Washington than walking around circles and houses like these—looking at places other people lived. The glimpse of mantelpieces, chandeliers, gardens, tree-lined blocks on winter nights, was something even my landlord liked. The odd thing was that someone who lived in one of these houses should still envy others, though what he envied most was, I suspect, not merely the real estate. "Frank's so lucky to have the Lug," my landlord said one evening when we passed Frank's building and I glanced up at his window, high up in the trees.

Often he would ask me in a wistful way about Frank and his boyfriend when we were making small talk in the kitchen—evidently this couple was in my landlord's eyes a sort of ideal. He had known Frank's boyfriend for years, had always found him attractive; he said when the Lug was living in the neighborhood, people had followed him home from the grocery store, he was so good-looking. It had taken Frank six years to even speak to him. Now they were together, a fixed star to be looked up at from the open sea of my landlord's idealism. Walking south on Fourteenth Street we stopped—at the glass doors of a sex club I went to on Thursday nights (half price for men thirty-five and up). "The last time I went here," my landlord said, "I was downstairs in the basement standing in a puddle of goo, while some guy chewed on my nipple, and I heard a little voice say: 'After so many deaths, you're still doing this?' "

That was the question—though I still walked over on Thursday evenings to the club—if only to look at the men in their towels, as artfully arranged (in pornographic poses) in their little cubicles as paintings at the National Gallery. He would not go to the sex club, I suspected, because too many people would recognize him there; I did not have this constraint. Yet, though I still went, my landlord and I had much in common: our age, our solitary status, the fact that we had survived something so many friends of ours had not. That was one reason no doubt I simply walked around the halls but never touched a human being: the presence of the dead. I continued going to the club but I never said so to my landlord. Then one day while looking through the scrapbooks in his study I came upon the photograph of a man I'd known in New York who was dead, a friend who had grown up in Washington. The next evening I asked, when my landlord and I met in the dining room, if he had known this person. "Of course!" my landlord said. "Everyone knew Nick."

"He was," I said. "He was so—"

"Genuine," my landlord said.

The word startled me; not just because it was so apt, but because it was, I suspected, the one thing my landlord and I were not, not only because I was not telling him I went to the club on Fourteenth Street.

"I still speak to his mother," he said. "She came to me when Nick was dying. I was working for the Social Security Administration then. She came to see me about getting Social Security for Nick. She waited all day, I remember, and finally she got to see me, and the minute she said her name, I said, 'I know your son,' and her face lighted up. 'You know my son?' she said. She was so relieved—she'd found a friend in the bureaucracy. I call her up every now and then and we go to the movies. She lives in the Westchester, this huge apartment complex on the way to your school. You must walk by it when you go to class. How is class, by the way?" he said cheerfully.

Class was strange, I told him—walking back I felt so drained by the seminar on Literature and AIDS, all I wanted to do was get home and lie down. The reason I said was this: That I was sitting in a room once a week at a long table talking about something that for these students was simply a historical event being studied in a seminar made me recall, as I led the discussion, all the people who were no longer alive. Here I am, I frequently thought, sitting in a seminar in Washington, D.C., twenty years later, discussing as a historical event the thing that killed my friends. The students looked at me across the table, I presumed, because I was older, had been out in the world, knew something they did not—but often, in the middle of the winter afternoon, I would watch their lips moving with such a surreal feeling inside as they discussed these texts by authors no longer on earth, that I found myself thinking: *I wonder when they will look up across the table and discover that their teacher is also dead.*

"Exactly," said my landlord.

Their open, glistening faces seemed so far removed from the actual events, I wondered why they were taking the course at all. Some spoke eagerly, with a loquacity that comes from that time in life when all one has to do is sing, like a bird on a perch, about what one has read, while Pop pays the bill. A few hardly said a word—uncomfortable, I imagined, with the homosexual content of the reading material, though one never knows the reason for the bored, dyspeptic expression on a student's face. His car may just have broken down, his computer crashed, his landlord kicked him out, his girlfriend left him; the students were involved in their own dramas. But I assumed it was the course material. The matter-of-fact way in which homosexual narratives were discussed by most students, however, without the blinking of an eye, shocked me. Homosexuality had been linked to liberal traditions of enlightenment and tolerance; it was now an accepted part of

American culture—the ongoing extension of freedom to include more and more groups, the package a college provided the middle-class student so that he or she could live successfully with "diversity"—though I never relinquished the suspicion that the audience was being politically correct. *Their real thoughts involve disgust,* I would always think as I walked home through the winter darkness, eager to get back to my room upstairs in the house on N Street, and the letters of a woman looking for a treatment at a spa that would relieve her spinal pain.

"AIDS is over," I told them one afternoon. "At least in this country—it had its cultural moment, and produced some art that will probably last no longer than thirties agit-prop. It galvanized the nation for a brief period, but that moment is past. There is still no cure, and people are still going to die, and it still interferes with sex, but when the public learned that it was not going to affect them, that it was mainly a gay disease, it moved on."

The faces round the table faced me with a glassy blankness—I didn't know if they knew I was being ironic—or if I knew myself. As I talked I split in two: the voice issuing from my lips, the rest of me watching them. One handsome student, with brown hair so thick it grew down his forehead like a wolf's, sat directly opposite me, his mouth growing more set, his expression colder, as I talked—till I mentioned a novel from the seventies that had been dismissed by a review claiming its gay characters were motivated entirely by Lust, at which point he said: "Well, weren't they?"

"No," I said. "I believe that each time they went out, even if it seemed to be about sex, it was never just about that. They were looking for Love. They may not have known it, or thought so, but in the end, that's what it was."

"But then why were they so promiscuous?"

"They thought they could get Love from sex!"

"But sex gave them AIDS!" he said.

"But they didn't know that," I said. "It was being spread when no one knew it existed."

"But they should have known!"

"That's like saying Lincoln went to Ford's Theatre the night he was shot knowing that's what would happen," I said. "Actually he was quite aware of the possibility that it might. But he went anyway. He went and it did happen. And that left everyone else to deal with it—which is what AIDS literature is all about."

The student regarded me with an even colder expression. "I don't see how you can compare Lincoln's assassination and AIDS," he said.

"They were both to a degree accidents," I said. "From the viewpoint of the person harmed—the person who did not desire this fate. That's all."

"Lincoln had just saved the Union," said the student. "People who died of AIDS had just had sex!"

"Then let's compare AIDS," I said, "to the Spanish influenza that killed millions of people after World War I."

"You don't get the flu by having sex," he said.

"I always do," Frank said, applying ChapStick to his lips as we drove back together after class that night. "And that's why you should get a flu shot. As for his views on AIDS—they don't surprise me in the least. I've asked those questions myself—and so have you. In fact, I told the Lug he had to get tested, and I had to see the results—in writing! He was quite offended. But I can't fool around—though I still wonder if I should even be proceeding with this relationship," he said, turning to me at a red light. "Do you know what he gave me for my birthday last week? A Time-Life geological time line of the United States! He puts a ski cap on when he goes to bed, no matter how hot it is. Plus he gets up every Sunday morning while I'm still asleep and goes to the Museum of Natural History. He was a drill sergeant in the Army for eight years. He eats tuna out of the can. He reads travel guides—but never goes anywhere. He's obsessed with the Civil War and slavery. He classifies people as humans, chimpanzees, or dogs."

"Why them?" I said.

"He says people are like chimps because they gossip—did you know that gossip, scientists now think, is just a human version of grooming, picking lice out of each other's heads, a social activity that bonds us?—and because chimps are so volatile, emotional, quick to anger, and in love with bright, shiny objects—and mean. As for dogs, it's because some human beings require hierarchy in order to live. They need a top dog, they live in packs, they turn aggressive in a group! He loves animal psychology," he said, as we turned on to Rhode Island Avenue.

Sometimes the Lug was waiting at Frank's apartment when we got back—seated in an armchair, reading one of his travel guides. He never said hello; it was as if we had not been out of the room at all. "I've decided where you should go on your next trip," he said to me when we walked in that night. "Mongolia." He looked up with his thin-lidded blue eyes. "They have yaks. And yak butter. You can hike up to fifteen thousand feet, and sleep in huts with a view of Everest. It's not as touristed as Tibet. And I have another place for you," he said. "Venezuela. A desert-like coast that alternates with jungle-covered islands at Los Roques. These weird plateaus that rise up from the ground in sheer cliffs called *tepuis*. W. H. Hudson wrote *Green Mansions* after seeing the *tepuis*."

"So why haven't you gone there yourself?" I said.

"Because I had no one to go with till now," said the Lug. "And I refuse to travel alone. And I'm afraid to fly. Seriously, if I were you, I'd go to Venezuela. After seeing the *tepuis* you can go to Angel Falls. Then there's the *llano*, the great grassy plain, and the border country with Brazil.

These places are changing rapidly," he said in an urgent tone—the voice of the sergeant he had once been talking to his trainees. "Tourism, mass tourism, is now the number one industry in the world. The rain forest is being decimated daily by unscrupulous loggers and poor farmers using slash-and-burn agriculture to grow cocaine for drug-hungry Americans. It's not going to be around much longer. People are destroying the planet—like locusts."

"I thought you said they were like chimpanzees," said Frank. "Or dogs."

"Those too," he said.

He returned to the subject later in Frank's apartment after we'd come back from dinner and he was leaving, his hand on the doorknob.

"Don't forget Venezuela," he said. "You can visit Lake Maracaibo, a shallow inland sea from which they get most of their oil. Then there's the *tepuis*, and Caracas, and Angel Falls. I'd like to see Angel Falls myself."

"Well, why don't you?" I said.

"Because I have to work! I'm a wage slave," he said, opening the door.

"Before you go, would you answer a question?" I said. "Do you think homosexuals are motivated entirely by Lust?"

"I'd have to think about that," he said. And he was gone.

Frank sighed. "I asked him that same question on Sunday. And do you know what he said?"

"What?"

As he started to speak the door reopened. "It depends on whether the homosexual is a chimpanzee, a dog, or a person," said the Lug. "If he's a person, he has higher needs than just an orgasm." Then the door closed.

Frank turned to me and said: "Last Sunday he asked me if I would ever leave him, and I said I thought he would probably leave me, and he said he'd never. That's my main anxiety, of course—being left."

"But you won't be," I said.

"I'd like to believe you," he said, "because I'm terrified of being abandoned. I must be special—to one person. Otherwise, frankly, I don't see the point. I've felt that way ever since my mother died. When your parents die, you know, your audience is gone. You really have no one who cares about what you do. But I think somebody has to care about you—someone has to think you matter."

"Can't you live on having mattered to someone?" I said.

"No—you can't live in the past. You only have this moment—though Americans, for some reason, seem incapable of living in the present. I don't even think they like life. Gay men especially won't let themselves be happy. Gay men are always punishing themselves."

"Whatever for?"

"For being gay! Sometimes I look over at him when he's in bed next to me and think—how did I get him? It's nothing I deserve—he's so beautiful!"

"My landlord would certainly agree," I said.

"Wonderful," said Frank. "If your friends don't want your boyfriend, what's the point? Now kiss Mother good night, she's exhausted."

And we exchanged two big air kisses, far from each other's cheeks, since Frank was afraid of germs and even carried around a bottle of disinfectant with which he immediately sprayed his hands after leaving someone.

When I got back to the house I did what people often do who have not had sex—ate something sweet: there, in the silence of the darkened house I sat at the dining room table and ate ice cream. I was still there when to my surprise my landlord came downstairs in his blue and white robe and slippers. I told him I'd compared AIDS to Lincoln's assassination, to no effect, in class, and he asked me if I was still reading Mrs. Lincoln's letters.

I told him I had just read a letter she had written Mrs. Keckley (her best friend at the time, a seamstress and former slave who made her dresses) about a train ride she had taken to Chicago after the doomed attempt to sell her clothes, and I picked up the book and opened it to read aloud. She was traveling, I said, as she sometimes did after the assassination, under an assumed name ("I am booked Mrs. Clarke; *inquire for no other person*."). The newspapers were denouncing her for the clothes sale, and when she finally found a seat on the crowded train ("I found, after you left me, I could not continue in the car in which you left me, owing to every seat's berth being engaged; so, being simple *Mrs. Clarke*, I had to eat 'humble pie' in a car less commodious.") it was behind two men who, as she sat there, began to argue about her attempt to sell her clothes. One of the men said she was crazy, the other said it was not her fault and that she had to go on living and had put up with a great deal. (Said one: "I do not blame her for selling her clothing, if she wishes it. I suppose *when sold* she will convert the proceeds into five-twenties to enable her to have means to be buried." Second man, "with the haughtiest manner": "That woman is not dead yet.") Then she went into the dining room and was ushered to a table, "where, at its head, sat a very elegant-looking gentleman . . . My black veil was doubled over my face. I had taken my seat next to him—he at the head of the table, 1 at his left hand. I immediately felt a pair of eyes was gazing at me. I looked him full in the face, and the glance was earnestly returned. I sipped my water, and said, 'Mr. Sumner, is this indeed you?' His face was as pale as the table-cloth . . . He said, 'How strange you should be on the train and I not know it!' "

"How strange indeed," murmured my landlord.

"Considering the senator from Massachusetts had come to the White House so frequently," I said, looking up from the book, "and been part of Mrs. Lincoln's inner circle, and then not seen her since the assassination. That's why their reunion was so painful—in fact, Mrs. Lincoln pretended she had to visit a sick friend to get away from him. Back to the letter." I resumed reading Mrs. Lincoln's words: "As soon as I could escape from the table, I did so by saying, 'I must secure a cup of tea for a lady friend with me who has a head-ache.' I had scarcely returned to the car, when he entered it with a cup of tea borne by his own aristocratic hands."

" 'His own aristocratic hands,' " said my landlord.

"I was a good deal annoyed by seeing him," I read, "and he was so agitated that he spilled half of the cup over my *elegantly gloved* hands. *He* looked very sad . . . His heart was in his eyes, notwithstanding my veiled face. Pity for me, I fear, has something to do with all this. I never saw his manner so gentle and sad . . . What evil spirit possessed me to go out and get that cup of tea? When he left me, *woman-like* I tossed the cup of tea out of the window, and tucked my head down and shed *bitter tears* . . ." I looked up. "He was so upset he spilled a cup of tea on her," I said, "and she burst into tears after he left her compartment."

"What a scene in a movie that would make!" said my landlord. He gazed into the garden. "Why has no one written an opera on this woman? Do you know what was written on the inside of her wedding ring?"

"Yes," I said.

"*Love Is Eternal,*" he said.

Her presence in the world after the assassination was so strange, I said. She was a ghost, a reminder of something the country wanted to put behind it. In some profound way she did not know what to do with herself, I said as my landlord got up and began to pace the room. She seemed to want to both live and die. She seemed to both hate and love attention. One time, I said, she was coming back from Europe when the ship pitched and she was nearly thrown down a flight of stairs, but a woman put her hand out and saved her life just in time. "It was Sarah Bernhardt!" said my landlord in a grave voice. "Who said she wondered, after Mrs. Lincoln identified herself, if she had done her a favor at all! Such was the grief that must have emanated from her."

He then finished the story: how, when the ship docked in New York, the reporters mobbed Bernhardt and ignored Mrs. Lincoln entirely; how she stood in the shadows watching the hubbub until Bernhardt and the reporters had left. "*The wheel of fortune!*" my landlord said. "The assassination destroyed her—it destroyed everyone who was in the box at the theater that night—one way or another."

"Real catastrophes, horrible accidents, always do," I said. "They affect not only the person who is actually hurt, but those around them. When some terrible misfortune happens it's not just the victim who suffers. There's a ripple effect. Everyone around the victim is affected."

"That's what happened to her," he said slowly as he stopped before the glass doors and looked out into the backyard. "When she died, the minister said she and Lincoln had been like two pine trees whose roots were intertwined—when lightning struck the one, the other only seemed to have survived, but it was dead too. That's why what Lincoln said to her the day he died is so sad. They'd gone out riding in a carriage to the Navy Yards and started talking about what they'd do now that the war was over, and Lincoln said they'd been through some dark times and should try to be happy now. Then he got the bullet," he said. "And her life ended too. The rest was just waiting—and the waiting, she said, was so long."

"Which is how people feel when people they love die," I said. "That they are only marking time. That their lives have ended. Like Henry Adams—after his wife killed herself he went on living. He traveled, he moved into the home they had just had built, he wrote books. But when someone asked him to speak to a historical society years later, he turned and said, 'But didn't you know? I've been dead for fifteen years.'"

"*But didn't you know? I've been dead for fifteen years!*" my landlord said.

"And during those years no one was allowed to even mention her name! By the time someone did, finally—the young woman they'd hired to take care of him near the end of his life—he said: 'My child, you have broken a silence of thirty years.'"

"*You have broken a silence of thirty years!*"

"Then when he died," I said, "this young woman went downstairs to look for his burial instructions, and what did she find in his desk drawer? The capsule of cyanide his wife had used to kill herself! I must go see that monument he built for her, by the way, the one by Saint-Gaudens. He used to sit there with the young woman who broke the silence by asking about his wife."

"You mean the monument in Rock Creek Cemetery. I've been *many* times," my landlord said. "Eleanor Roosevelt used to go there by herself after she found out Franklin had a mistress, when she thought her world had come to an end."

"Life's rotten," I said.

"Yes, it is," he said. "It's like a boxing match—you go out into the ring, and dance around, and then you get hit, and then again, and then again, and by the time the round is over, I imagine most people are ready to quit. But that's why we have an obligation to make it as pleasant as possible—despite everything! We have an obligation to live in the present—to be happy now!"

An obligation more easily honored in the breach than the observance, said Frank. Though the discovery that my landlord knew even more about Mrs. Lincoln than I did, and appreciated her deeply, made me feel an even greater bond with him, I continued to walk to the White House by myself every night, to stand in Lafayette Square, then walk home through remarkably empty streets. Frank called when the weather was fine and told me to meet him in Dupont Circle—on the inner circle of benches, around the fountain, though I preferred the outer, where one felt less conspicuous—and we sat there watching people. ("You're only as old as your hair," Frank would say. "That's the sad truth, I'm afraid.") Watching was not all we did; frequently one of Frank's friends came up to chat. "Nice to meet you," I would say when the friends left while Frank removed from his pocket the small bottle of antibacterial lotion, which he sprayed on his hands after they walked off. ("You can't be too careful in this city, you know.") But in truth I was usually too gloomy to sit there very long, watching the parade of people. Walking alone was the only thing that relieved my mood. The longest walk was to and from school. When our schedules matched, Frank would give me a ride, in one or both directions, but mostly I walked. Walking up in daylight, there was traffic and the occasional pedestrian to deal with; walking home after class, I had the whole journey to myself—uphill to the National Cathedral, then down Massachusetts Avenue to Sheridan Circle, then past the spot before the Irish embassy where the Chilean diplomat Orlando Letelier had been assassinated, down Nineteenth to N Street: a long gentle descent to town. At the entrance to the vice president's compound—blocked permanently by a parked car—there was a sign that gave the hour, minute, second, and hundredth of a second in Greenwich Mean Time. It was followed by the long stretch bordered by the fir trees of his estate, and then the British embassy, and then Brazil's, and then the Japanese, in whose backyard the staff had been found burning papers after Pearl Harbor, then Korea, Mexico, Cote d'Ivoire, Egypt, Ireland, Greece, and Luxembourg, and finally the house on N Street, and the closed doors of my landlord's study, with the light shining around the edges.

It was nice to come back to a house in which one did not live alone, I told Frank one evening. Frank agreed. When Nureyev went back to Russia, he said, he was accosted by an old woman who asked him, "Where is home for you?" And Nureyev said: "Home? What is home?" And the babushka replied: "Where someone waits for you." Frank turned to me. "Pow! Wham! Right on the kisser!" he said. "Leave it to a babushka to get right to the heart of the matter!" Of course my landlord wasn't waiting for me exactly; but he was there behind the study doors when I climbed the stairs. It seemed to me that was almost enough. Then one morning when I came down I found he'd left the local gay newspaper on the dining room table with a personal ad circled in red ink. "Fun, outgoing, fiftysomething," it read, "considered attractive, non-smoker, financially solid, old-fashioned but zany, likes to discuss politics and the Broadway stage, seeks same, or younger, sense of humor a plus, Dupont Circle area."

"Fun! Outgoing! Fiftysomething!" Frank said, when I read it aloud in the car on our way to work. "Please! The basic template for a personal ad is 'Raging size queen seeks more, better!' This is the sort of ad you get from a Baptist. And what does a Baptist really want? The Antichrist! But of course he can't possibly let someone like that in the house! Hence the ad—a mere gesture, to alleviate his growing fear that he might as well sit by the window with his dog and wave at passersby. Oh, forgive me," he said, "that's what you do."

"Do you think he'll have any luck?" I asked.

"Who knows?" Frank said. "People are such snobs! I'm always trying to fix my unattached friends up with perfectly attractive men, but the moment I tell them who exactly I have in mind, they say: 'That old thing? She's older than I am!' I think it's admirable of him to place the ad at all."

He met respondents to his ads in the hotel on Nineteenth Street—in a lobby whose chairs were set against a glass wall so close to the sidewalk the people sitting there looked like insects in a terrarium. I would see him there some nights on my way home from school—listening with a judicial air to a man in the chair across from him present his case, like two businessmen negotiating an oil-and-gas deal. An hour later, back at the house, I would hear him return home, and open the refrigerator so he could sit there in the dark gnawing on some chicken part. One evening I asked my landlord how his last interview had gone. He stopped on his way up the stairs. "He practically needed a walker!" he said. The next time it was: "He was perfectly fine except he disapproves of the Clintons—and I am not about to date a Republican!" And finally, one night, pausing on the stairs: "Oh, you know," he said in a tired voice. "He knew my story, and I knew his!" Then he laughed and went up to his room.

He began leaving the study doors open now, however, while he worked—he seemed to have accepted my presence—and I could pause on my way up to banter with him about these attempts as I stood just outside the doorway.

"It's obvious what his problem is," said Frank, lighting a cigarette one day on our way to work. "He's still looking for the hot number—but the hot number is thirty-five."

"Oh, right," I said.

"But, like all of us, he's aging. The nictitating membrane is starting to descend! And you know what that brings—complete occlusion! Oblivion and night!"

One morning I came downstairs and found him to my surprise still at the dining room table in his bathrobe, with circles under his eyes and disheveled hair.

"I didn't sleep a wink last night," he said. "Not a wink."

"Why not?"

"I was thinking about my parents. They both just had cataract operations, my mother has started to fall down, and forget things, my father has a heart murmur and is going deaf. Last night on the phone I mentioned the Pan Am Building in New York and he thought I'd said the Canned Ham Building. I think I may have to move them up here, to make sure they're all right. They were there for me, and I'm going to be there for them. I'm not going to let them down. I'm not going to let them down," he said. He stood up and put his glass of orange juice on the counter. He looked out at the garden. Then he turned to me and said: "You know, you learned a lot that gay life cannot teach you by taking care of your mother." Then he went upstairs. Moments later he came down dressed for work, the moment of intimacy gone. "I've got to get to the office," he said in a hearty voice. "But it's Sunday!" I said. "I know," he said, "but I've got a deadline tomorrow—that regulation subheading on what size truck tires a corporation can use to inspect water levels in the mines, you know, is crucial to America's future!" Then he asked me where I was headed.

"The Mall," I said. "There's a lecture in the National Gallery at noon."

"On what?" said my landlord.

"Two marine landscapes by a French painter of the eighteenth century."

"I used to go to those," he said. "A lot—and then I stopped."

"Why?"

"Because one day I looked around me at the other people. Have you ever looked at the other people?"

"Not really," I said.

"Well, next time, do," he said. "Going to those lectures

does something to the face." He laughed. "Have you been to the Renwick?"

"What's that?" I said.

"It's that Second Empire wedding cake across from the Executive Office Building," he said. "It was built in 1861 by a very rich man named Corcoran, and inside it still has an atmosphere that will make you feel you're at one of Mrs. Lincoln's soirees," he said. "Potted palms and poufs. Very nineteenth century. Or go to the National Museum of American Art—where Lincoln had his inaugural ball, and Whitman took care of wounded soldiers during the war. There's a room on the second floor, at the northeast corner, you should see. In it you'll find two stained-glass windows by John La Farge, and a painting by Abbott Thayer, who was famous for painting angels, and a portrait of a man in a white linen suit with a cat in his lap who looks completely gay. The whole room is like a funeral chapel. Very Pre-Raphaelite, very fin de siècle. They were all preoccupied with the Middle Ages, with lilies and angels and Death, those people—for good reason. They'd gone through the Civil War."

I stood there for a moment watching him run his fingertips across his moustache, while the handsome veteran with the battered face picked up leaves off the sidewalk, one by one, and put them in his pocket.

"Why do we care about the past?" I said.

"Because it gives some dignity to our paltry little lives,"

said my landlord. Then he looked away. "Well, have a good one!" he said in his hearty, cheerful voice, and he walked off.

At the Renwick I found just what he promised: potted palms, upholstered settees, statues like *Boy with a Thorn*, and paintings hung one on top of the other from floor to ceiling the way they had been in the nineteenth century. Several were big landscapes by people like Bierstadt of that part of the country where Lincoln thought he might like to live after he left the White House: the West. One could imagine for a moment the raffish little salon Mrs. Lincoln, always receptive to a European title and gossip about European courts, had gathered in the White House—several of whose members had betrayed her when trouble came. Then I walked past the big white house they had both ended up hating down to the Mall. There were several options there. There were Marie Antoinette's earrings and a giant squid to look at in the Museum of Natural History; there was Mary Lincoln's dress in the Museum of American History; there were Persian manuscripts, and silver ewers from the Sassanian dynasty in the Sackler, and Chinese bronzes and scrolls at the Freer, and modern art at the Hirshhorn, but the museum I wound up at that day was the National Gallery.

The minute I entered the National Gallery I felt safe. Nothing bad could happen here, I thought, no ugliness intrude. Everything that made life awful had been banished.

No one even aged. The flowers in the Dutch still lifes, no matter how many symbolic items had been included to remind us of mortality—the decomposing bread, the fly in the jam, the skull, the dead fish—were always blooming. No one would decompose, or sicken, or die—the only organic thing in the whole building (besides the people looking at the paintings) were the flowers that they put around the pool. It was like being in a temple—it was modeled on the Pantheon in Rome, after all, and, sitting on a bench in the rotunda watching the people go by, one could have been in some idealized whatever waits for us beyond the grave.

That day I left the museum when it closed, sat on a bench on the Mall to kill time, and went back when it reopened an hour later for the concert they gave every Sunday night at seven o'clock. On Sunday night the National Gallery was really like a tomb: entering on Massachusetts Avenue through the great bronze doors when it was already dark, walking up the stairs into the hushed rotunda. Even the light was dimmer; the flowers around the pool sad-looking in the deserted gloom, the only sound the squeak of your shoes as you walked the long corridor to the courtyard at the western end. My landlord had told me about these concerts too: I was walking around a Washington he had long since apparently discarded. Otherwise I'd never have known one could be in the museum after closing. It was an experience I treasured. One could not look at the paintings, and a guard stood in the rotunda to make sure you did not try. The galleries were blocked by wooden partitions, as if the paintings were asleep, like children who have been put to bed. The courtyard I finally entered was just as somnolent. With its wan light and tall, thin, feathery palms almost touching the concave skylight, its columns and plashing fountain, one expected to see women stretched out in long white gowns on the wrought-iron chairs, like the woman in the John Singer Sargent painting called *Repose*, looking bored and exhausted. Instead there was a hodgepodge of people in everything from T-shirts to coats and ties sitting on folding chairs as they examined their programs.

The people who had come here to listen to the concert, especially those who had found spots on the benches along the wall, looked more like pilgrims at Lourdes, or pale plants seeking the light in a rain forest where, in the depths of winter, lilies were blooming—though here the palms raised their feathery arms into a birdless atmosphere that could never threaten them with a storm or wind, but only the limitations of the space in which they grew, since some of them were about to touch the skylight now: a metaphor for Washington, I thought, where life was so comfortable because it was so artificial, as if we were all living under a glass roof, or in some parlor where a body was laid out amidst the lilies.

The performers alone seemed to possess energy—even

though most nights it seemed they were expending it on perversely obscure works, performing everything but the music the composer was famous for—as if, given the fact that this was a free concert, they might as well play music they couldn't elsewhere. Often the pianist or violinist asked the composer—a professor he or she had studied with—to stand and bow after the premiere of some sonata. At almost every concert, however, no matter how irritating, there was one piece—sometimes only a passage—that made you feel you'd done the right thing in coming here; that someone else (the composer) had understood, had known, your grief, that life was worth living because of music. At the same time, this music, or piece of music, also made it clear that you had been fooling yourself in attempting to go on with your life; that what had happened to the person you loved you would never get over; that you still carried it with you; that it lay beneath all things; and only this music—these few notes—recognized that everything else you had been doing, and would do, to fill up the time was meaningless. Then the passage ended, and you looked around, at the other people listening, and finally the solitary young man a few rows in front of you biting his nails, or the man next to him looking at his watch.

Walking home after the concert I had the Mall all to myself, a cleansing half hour that ended with regret when I had to turn at Fourteenth Street and enter the city of concrete and asphalt—but then there was the darkness of

Lafayette Square, the sound of the White House fountain splashing, and finally the emptiness of Connecticut Avenue on a Sunday night. Most cities are deserted on Sunday nights; everyone has gone to bed. If on my way upstairs I found my landlord working in his study with the doors open I would tell him about the concert; he'd listen, smiling, but he never went. All the things I was doing were things he'd done so many years ago they were not subject to resuscitation. I kept going back to the museum, however, every Sunday night; because it both deepened and relieved my solitude—and weekdays, too. Sometimes I'd see the same guard who'd worked overtime at the concert standing in a gallery the next day, and feel embarrassed, as if only anonymity permitted me to be such a museum addict. On weekends, the place could be so crowded that when you entered, the air seemed humid with human perspiration. During the week, however, the museum had an atmosphere so still, so vacant, the silence in these rooms was strangely enervating, and the longer you stayed, the more exhausted you got, like a patient whose staying in bed actually fatigues him. But I went down almost every day, often to look at something my landlord had told me about that I would have never noticed myself: the small room with American trompe l'oeils, the even smaller room with the Dutch flower paintings. That winter they were renovating the skylights, and the paintings in the rooms did not correspond to the floor plan in the brochure given out at

the entrance desk. Because of that I often got lost and found myself in rooms with pictures I would not have made a point to look at otherwise. Upstairs only the Italian paintings were where they were supposed to be— including a room full of Titians, in front of which there were two small sofas, back to back, I often used since I was usually tired when I got there—though it wasn't just the sofas that made me sit for a long time in front of those paintings; it was the paintings themselves, whose beauty seemed to grant the same relief the occasional passage of music did.

It was a room, really, devoted to sexual vanity—not just the amour propre that leads people (a doge, a cardinal, a general, a lady) to be painted in all their robes and armor and trappings of wealth, but the specific need to be desired. In one painting, Venus is looking at herself in a mirror; in another she is trying to detain Adonis from leaving her bed—though it isn't exactly a bed, but rather a red robe on which Venus sits outdoors in the forest, her bare legs, buttocks, and back leading the eye up to the central image in the painting, her arms outstretched around her lover's chest—while smooth-skinned Adonis, already dressed, is striding away, holding in his right hand the staff that will help him walk out of the picture frame as quickly as he can, and in his left the leashes of his large dark dogs. It's a somber painting, whose darkness only deepens when you look closer and see the faces of the pair: Venus in the

shadow of her lover's torso, gazing up at him with both despair and panic, all conveyed by the whites of her eyes, while Adonis looks down at her with a certain irritation and contempt. Though there are a rainbow and a Cupid and a burst of light in the upper-right-hand corner, the white limbs are set against colors that are mostly dark green and brown, and the painting could not be more portentous: it is the moment we all fear, the moment of abandonment, when even after the most intimate of acts, you are left behind, with the torture of unsatisfied desire—the longing for more of the bliss you have just tasted, a bliss brought to you by a person who is moving on to something or someone else. That's at least how I used to interpret the scene—till one day I was sitting before the picture, studying the expression on Adonis's face, when into the room walked the young man who had asked during the seminar on AIDS if all homosexuals were not motivated by Lust. I had not even time to say hello before he came right over to the sofa, sat down, and said: "So tell me why you like this painting."

"Probably," I said, "because there's a sofa in front of it."

"No, really!" he said.

"Well," I said, "it's not my favorite picture in this room. But I guess it's the situation—it's a very human moment, wouldn't you say? In fact, I've always thought there should be a caption underneath this painting that says 'Don't leave me this way'—do you know that old song

from the seventies? Or: 'Won't you at *least* give me your phone number?' "

I turned to him and smiled but got only a frown in return.

"But that isn't all that's happening," he said, wringing his hands as he leaned forward. "It's not that she's being abandoned. After all, she's Venus—she's an Immortal."

"The gods can suffer, too," I said. "They can fall in love with mortals."

"That's true," he said. "And in Ovid's myth, Venus was much more in love with Adonis than he was with her. He just wanted to go hunting. So she warned him not to hunt the dangerous animals, like boars and lions, because she knew they could kill him. But he wouldn't listen. Then one day a boar did kill him and she found him lying in the forest, bleeding, and turned his blood into a flower we call the anemone. That's the real reason she's holding him back—not because she doesn't want to be dumped, but because she was afraid he would get killed. Which is what happened. The lesson of the myth is that Adonis refused Love—to go hunting," he said, sitting back. "Just like my brother."

"Your brother?" I said.

"My brother died of AIDS," he said. "He got it from the first man he ever slept with—a doctor in Berlin. He was living in Germany at the time—working with a dance company. I took care of him that whole summer. He never once complained," he said, his eyes suddenly glistening, the way grief can intrude with no forewarning into conventional moments. Then he told me about that summer in Berlin: walking around the city convinced there was a worm in his own bowels, getting tested himself every few days at different clinics, his brother's refusal to complain, their father's refusal to pay for the funeral, his mother's still going to the grave every day outside Toronto. "There's a version of this painting in the museum in Berlin," he said, pulling himself together. "I used to go there when my brother was sick to look at it." He continued to stare at the painting. "My brother was like Adonis," he said. "He looked like the Adonis in this painting. But not toward the end."

"I'm sorry."

"Yes, well," he said, "you have to move on."

"But you don't," I said. "You don't have to move on."

"Yes, you do. My brother would have wanted me to, I'm sure of that. My brother loved life. That's why he got killed." And with that he stood up, said good-bye, and walked out of the room. The museum guard in the corner—those inexplicable ciphers—announced the museum's closing in five minutes. I got up and walked through the galleries out onto the steps overlooking the Mall. But the student had disappeared. So I walked home by myself, thinking of all the things I should have said to him. When I got back I was glad to see my landlord sitting at the dining room table reading the newspaper and asked him how the latest respondent to his personal ad had gone.

"Oh," he said, "he was way too young. The trouble with the young is they all expect you to be Daddy."

He went to the French doors open to the garden and took a deep breath of the moist air. "But I don't want to be anyone's Daddy—not a tot from Uzbekistan, or a young man looking for the coach he saw in some porn film. I don't want to be Daddy. And when an evening like this comes along, *I* feel young. Doesn't this weather remind you of how you felt the first time you moved to a city?" he said. "When all you wanted to be was a white T-shirt in the dark? You know, I think that's what I'll do. I'm going to the Circle to be a T-shirt in the dark—want to come?"

I said I had to get some work done for school and went upstairs to think about the afternoon. The minute my landlord left I went to the study and freed the dog. She followed me to my room and lay down beside me. Then I fell asleep. When I awoke the dog was gone and I could hear a voice downstairs—I went out onto the landing and saw the dog greeting my landlord.

"How did she get out of the study?" he said when I got downstairs.

"I let her out so she could sit with me while I read," I said, putting on my coat as if nothing were the matter. "Then I fell asleep. Dogs are amazing." I walked to the door and unlocked it with my key. "I didn't even hear you come through the door but she did!"

He shook his head, like a parent disappointed in his

child's behavior, and walked upstairs with the dog beside him and a frown on his face.

I was so upset that when I entered Dupont Circle and saw Frank sitting on a bench smoking a cigarette I sat down beside him and explained what had happened. He said nothing but I went on defending myself. "It's bad enough the dog has to stay there all day while he's at work," I said, "but at night when it's pitch-black in that room I think it's cruel. Why should any living thing have to stay in a dark room all by herself?"

"Because the dog rips up the upholstery," he said, tapping the ash off his cigarette. "He told you. Furniture is furniture! Besides, dogs like a sense of structure. Literally. They like to be confined—they feel secure, in their own little space. They want boundaries."

"I know, but—"

"No, *I* know," he said. "You thought how nice it could be—the two of you together in that house—how well you get along, how considerate he is, how similar your lives. I realize your heart is like a little ship, looking for safe harbor. I understand that you developed habits of intimacy with your mother that you'd now like to transfer to another human being. I suppose you want to be needed, to be useful, to someone else. I understand the way a tenant can think himself more than a tenant. But, darling, get a grip! The study doors will always be closed!" And with that he threw his cigarette down and walked off.

A homeless man across from me was sitting up, perhaps reflecting on the day's events, before putting himself into the horizontal position his confreres had assumed on the adjacent benches. I jumped up from my bench and walked back down New Hampshire Avenue to O Street, past the mansion people rented for parties and receptions, the trees in front of it always strung with white lights no matter what the season, then the town house in which Jesse Jackson Jr. reportedly lived, and then the mews, and then the street with the little movie theater and then my landlord's block. To my horror when I rounded the corner, the house was pitch-black. It was like the house I returned to the day my mother died: empty in a way it had never been before.

The next day I was reading Mary Lincoln's letters ("You should go out *every day* and enjoy yourself—you are so *very young* and should be as gay as a lark. Trouble comes soon enough, my dear child, and you must enjoy life, whenever you can.") when my landlord walked up to the third floor and knocked on the wall beside my open door. "Come in!" I said, but he remained outside in the hall. He wanted to let me know he was taking a brief trip to a coal mine in Colorado. He went there once a year, he said; he would be leaving the following afternoon after work. That morning I went into the study after he left for the office. On a hassock were the things he had laid out for his journey—his plane ticket and passport, and several vials of pills. One of them was labeled with the name of a medicine people with AIDS took. But after looking at it closer, I concluded it was something a person who did not have HIV could take for other reasons. Then I went to his desk to examine the papers there. All I found there that day was a pamphlet that purported to show that, contrary to other claims, the Bible had nothing to say about homosexuality as we know it and therefore contained nothing that condemned it.

An hour later I was still in the study looking at his scrapbooks when the phone rang, and I listened to my landlord's bright, husky voice asking the caller to leave a message (". . . and I'll get right back to you! Thanks, and have a nice day!"), and then a woman began to speak in a weak, tired voice, "Hi, it's your mother! Just wanted to say thank you for the articles you sent, and the box of chocolates. It was just like you. I appreciate it. We love you!"

An obscene message could not have shocked me more. My landlord was loved—by his parents. That was what explained his incorrigible aloofness—that exasperating mixture of friendliness and distance. They were the only people who mattered to him really. That huge network of friends was not really a family: they were, contrary to sitcoms on TV, just friends. As I looked around the comfortable room, while the little radio on the table by the window played at a volume barely audible to human ears, the dog following me with her eyes, the study seemed even emptier than ever, for all its personal possessions. It was a relief to leave the house for school.

I started walking a few hours early up Massachusetts Avenue in a state of deep dejection. It was a long walk and there was too much time to think on it, and thinking always made me turn over in my mind the deaths of people I had loved. Was it true, as the nurse had said, that families keep their loved ones alive even when the loved ones wish to go? Was that the dark, the nightmare, side of loving care? Had my father asserted himself best of all by dying quickly within a week of his consignment to the same nursing home in which his wife had lived so many years? Was the whole thing an act of egotism on my part? Were we all simply afraid to die? Nowhere did I feel more certainly that everything I was doing was simply to kill time than on that walk to school. I envied my landlord his busy life. He seemed to at least have a certain animal vigor I felt least of all when I set out for school. The feeling of vacancy always intensified the hour it took to walk the gradual ascent to Ward Circle—in part because the weather was always mild, and flabby, in part because I was almost always alone on that sidewalk; so alone I looked forward to the man, halfway to school, who sometimes stood outside the Vatican embassy holding a sign that said PRIESTS MOLEST CHILDREN WORLDWIDE. The embassies showed not the slightest sign of life, while some of them seemed even shabby—and made one wonder how certain countries notorious for the poverty of their citizens could afford such grand, if dilapidated, Beaux-Art châteaux. There was something particularly shabby about several of these on close inspection, an abandoned air that matched my mood: garbage in the hedges, patches of dead grass, bars on the windows. Only Sheridan Circle was elegant: the Irish and Egyptian embassies, the house that Natalie Barney's sister had once owned, then blocks away the mosque whose minaret provided a landmark when one got lost in other parts of town, then the ravine of Rock Creek Park, then a slope that led to a statue of Winston Churchill and the British embassy, which looked like a high school built in the fifties, and then the Vatican embassy, whose patrician palazzo was mocked by the short, trim man who stood in front of it most days holding the sign. Often in my loneliness I would stop and talk to him, listening to his story about the priest who'd suggested something untoward on a ski trip to the Dolomites when he was only fifteen, and then, with one more lamentation added to the world, I'd leave him behind, ringing his bell, like a buoy in a fog warning ships of a rock, a sound that followed me halfway to the National Cathedral, where I sometimes turned onto Cathedral Avenue—and started down the hill past faux Tudor homes with apple trees in their yards, and then, in a ravine, the huge apartment houses people never had to leave if they did not wish to.

In one of the biggest of these—the one Barry Goldwater had lived in—lived the mother of the friend my landlord and I had in common, the one who'd died in 1983. Each time I passed the gates I told myself I should visit her, though, finding the thought of such a visit lugubrious (there was no reason I was calling on her except the fact that her son was dead), I always walked by her building without stopping—thinking, each time I did, that her son's last letter to me had been written when he could not sleep and was sitting on the john at four in the morning with diarrhea. That day I decided to visit her.

Thus do we remember the dead, I thought, and I turned in to the building grounds. A receptionist behind two glass doors buzzed me in after hearing via the intercom that I wished to see Mrs. Dixon. Inside, the lobby was virtually empty: a vast white marble room with just a semicircle of mailboxes, a single chair, and a table. The receptionist handed me the telephone; I introduced myself to Mrs. Dixon; she asked me if I would have dinner with her that evening, and I said yes. Then I left, feeling much better, and walked down to the bottom of the ravine, filled with woods, then more apartment buildings with swimming pools seen through the trees, still covered with tarpaulins, women walking their dogs on the sidewalk and a cluster of Central Americans, who seemed to be doing all the manual labor in Washington at this time in history, waiting for the bus; and finally up another hill, past a private elementary school where, every time I passed by, the children stood on the sidewalk corners, dressed as traffic guards, enjoying their ability to stop cars when someone wished to cross; and then the campus.

The English Department building, its windows glowing on top of the hill, always looked like an incubator in which eggs were being hatched under controlled light and humidity, but no matter how I felt when I arrived, walking down the corridor lined with glum students waiting on benches like patients about to receive the results of their CAT scans, my office mate was a lift. She always wore a beautiful scarf and earrings, her thick, wiry hair drawn back at the nape of her neck in an explosive ponytail. She was excited about getting tenure; waiting for her first book (*Laments and Longing in Nineteenth-Century American Literature*) to be reviewed; deciding whether or not the man she was dating should be the father of her children. She was always trying to fix me up—with a man in the church choir she belonged to, or someone in the Economics Department, or even the visiting poet that year, a big bald man my age who had lived in a small town in Ohio with his mother till her death the previous year, a man who had remained even more aloof from faculty life than I. "You must be a wonderful teacher," I said when I sat down that afternoon. "Whenever I come here, some young woman is sitting outside your door waiting to see you. They come to you like pilgrims going to Santiago de Compostela. What do you *do* for them?"

"Explain why I can't raise the grade on their last paper," she said. "That's the reason they come to see me. These kids are very practical."

"Then give me some practical advice," I said. "I'm going to see the mother of a friend of mine who died of AIDS. But I'm wondering if the thing to do is talk about her son, or not talk about him. Which do you think?"

"She'll let you know," she said. "Some people don't want to be reminded, and some people do. And now, before I go to class, you have to give me some advice. Do you like my hair this way," she said, loosening the rubber band so that her hair splayed out from her head, "or this?," pulling it back behind her again.

"They're both nice," I said.

"You should be more decisive," she said. "But thanks for the compliment. Well," she said, standing up and throwing her arms out, "it's showtime! Grief and Mourning in the Victorian Novel. I wonder if they'll have done even half the reading."

Hours later the day was fading, but I turned off the fluorescent light—so that the room filled with the gray twilight coming through the grimy windows—and went out into the hallway. The school was emptying. Inside the chilly men's room I found the windows open; someone was sitting in a stall, patiently waiting. On the wall beside the urinal was an advertisement for men who liked South Asians. I had no idea who was behind the closed door. On Saturday mornings a middle-aged man always stopped by this men's room, a baseball cap perched on his head at a jaunty angle, taking a tour of campus bathrooms on his day off, like a lobster fisherman checking his traps. The person in the stall had to be a student. But I did not have the time to find out. I washed my hands, got a drink of water, and went back to the office, now filled with a crepuscular gloom. I was glad to be alone. There was nothing more suitable to my spirits than the office after hours, when the building had emptied, and the fading light of a winter afternoon began to withdraw from the shelves of books—books on the Victorians, on feminism, romanticism, structuralism, post-structuralism, mourning, grief, and masochism, books that had been turned into another book (like my office mate's). I sat there for a while feeling this was where I'd like to live, in this office, and then got up to visit the men's room once more before leaving for good—and nearly collided with the visiting poet on his way out.

He glared at me with mournful eyes.

"How's it going?" I said.

"Okay," he said.

"I understand you live in a small town, too, in the country."

"Yeah," he said, and he went out the door.

It was then I decided to leave and walk down to see the mother of my old friend, even though it was still early. When one needed a mother, anyone's would do. To kill half an hour I watched some children playing soccer in the school playground at the top of the hill and then went down to the apartment complex on Cathedral Avenue. She came down to the lobby dressed in a white blouse with a broad collar, a black skirt, and a strand of imitation pearls; she did not want to ask me up to her apartment because it was still filled with boxes she had not unpacked since selling her house in Chevy Chase and moving here five years ago after her ex-husband's second wife cut her out of the will. Her gentle voice and smile, the slightly daffy air she had, reminded me of my friend. We walked through a long underground tunnel to another building whose lobby gave on to a large dining room. The room she led me into glowed a soft pink; my shoes sank into the thick carpet; the tables were covered with linen tablecloths, the butter lay in little squares atop piles of ice in silver urns. Walking past the sweating pitchers, the baskets of house rolls, we headed toward a table for two by the window, where, after sitting down, she removed her glasses from her handbag, and perused the menu silently, like a woman crossing the Atlantic on the old *Queen Mary*—something my friend had done often as a child, though when I knew him he was a penniless homosexual living in a high rise on the Lower East

Side of New York, trying to meet his rent by removing unwanted hair from men's backs with electrolysis.

His mother had the same placid, moonlike expression on her face that he had worn—the same smile, even the same gleaming white skin, the skin her son had carefully preserved by scrupulously avoiding the sun. I was used by now to finding my dead friends in their mothers when I finally met them. It was the case this time too. This was where he had got his complexion; the complexion he preserved so carefully in a world where everyone else seemed to insist on sunbathing. Even in summer I would see him walking down the beach on Fire Island, or the grimier sidewalk of Fourteenth Street, as white as cold cream under a straw hat. He wanted to be perfect—hence the removal of every hair on his torso by electrolysis, something he practiced on himself long before he thought of doing it on other people for money. After his death I had found myself in the Metropolitan Museum one day, in the room on the main floor full of fragments of Greek statues and their Roman copies, and thought of him—how white, how perfectly proportioned, his body had been. He was the only person I'd known who had stopped going to the gym because he did not want to get too big. He'd spent his days maintaining his proportions; preparing himself like a geisha for the rich men who'd once flown him to islands in the Caribbean with a host of health regimens that included sleeping under bug lights, drinking protein shakes, and never going out into the sun. Nor was this devotion to his body merely external. Even before AIDS he'd taken Diotoquin prophylactically in order to protect himself from amoebiasis, an occupational hazard of having sex in New York in those days, and read books on the power of the mind. By the time we met he'd become so poor he was living on food stamps—at which point he decided to change reality by learning to view it differently; which meant he took est, and Silva Mind Control, learned to walk on hot coals, and told us we were having no luck meeting people because we were "making things wrong" by being too critical. Then came the greatest challenge yet to viewing life correctly: he was told he had HIV.

A friend said he'd looked like a deer caught in a car's headlights for weeks after being told. He even chased the doctor who had given him the news into a grocery store on Second Avenue one day and stood there in Produce screaming at him that he was wrong. "I got what I resisted," he said before he died, in the same placid voice his mother used.

We did not talk about him until she picked her purse up from the floor and removed some photographs. There were two, taken when he was so ill he had moved back to Washington so she could care for him. One photograph showed my friend smiling a smile so appealing he did not even look ill; the other showed him in profile, gaunt and haunted, looking down at something outside the frame—contemplating his own death.

"He was too weak to carry his own suitcase when he got to Washington," she said when I handed back the photographs. "I had to drag it across the platform to the station. I told him, 'I haven't carried anything this heavy since I carried you.'" She picked up her purse and put the photographs inside. Then she looked out the window, through which, she said, she could often see deer on the lawn below. "Last night I heard a thud on the ceiling," she said to me in her soft voice, when she had put the purse back down, "and then nothing for a long time. I tapped on the ceiling but got no reply. I decided the man in the apartment above mine had fallen and I phoned 911, and sure enough, I was right. He'd had a stroke. He's in the hospital now."

She did not seem concerned about her own future though she was in her eighties; her main concern was still her son, whose end had not been pretty. All those hours in the gym, the omelets and alfalfa sprouts, the milk shakes filled with protein supplements, the avoidance of sunlight, the courses in mind control, the walking on coals, I thought, for naught—though I could see, talking to his mother, where he had got his belief in the power of the mind to control reality. She exuded the calm of a woman who regarded life in totally rational terms. So had her son—except he had taken this faith too far, it had seemed to us at the time, and granted the mind a power one en-countered mostly in comic books about heroes with X-ray vision. Now I sat listening to her talk about her dissertation on public education, and the work she had done in the schools around Washington, on subjects on which she was still consulted. She had the Washingtonian's rational faith that one could study a problem and solve it. So it was not a surprise when she told me, in passing, that there was no life after death. "You don't think we might wake up on the other side?" I said. "The way we wake up from a sleep?"

"No," she said in her soft voice, gently touching the sil-verware beside her plate. "People think that only because we do wake up from sleep, and they draw an analogy. But there's a very big difference. When we wake up from sleep, we are still alive, our bodies and brains are functioning and being fed blood. When we die, our bodies and brains have stopped. Hence there is no consciousness. Hence we cannot wake up. It's merely a false extrapolation people want to make because they cannot bear the thought of their own extinction."

"But then why," I said, "do people still feel the dead are with us? And why do we feel we have to apologize to them?"

"What do you mean?" she said.

"I'm reading the letters of Mary Todd Lincoln," I said. "And thinking about Henry Adams's wife, Clover—and the way both women were crushed by grief."

"Oh yes," she said. "Clover Adams adored her father—and nursed him when he was dying. Then she killed herself. But, you know, it ran in the family. Two of her brothers killed themselves, I believe. In fact, before Henry married her, Henry's brother warned him about her family's propensity for suicide."

"But she seems to have died of guilt," I said, "—which I think was Mary Todd Lincoln's case, too. That she had got her husband to the White House, that she had been ambitious for him—when her ambition seemed to have cost her everyone she loved. That's why she wore black for the rest of her life. The guilt was so deep. She dressed in mourning the rest of her life—as if she were performing penance, or branding herself. I think both women were crushed by guilt."

"Well, everyone feels guilty to some degree about surviving someone they love. It's like a doctor, I suppose, losing a patient. As if you could keep them alive forever. But of course you can't."

"But what if you . . . did sin?" I said.

"Did sin?" she said.

"Yes. How do you make amends when the person you wronged is dead?"

"I suppose by doing something good to those who are still alive. I think often of a line from Sophocles—we have all eternity to please the dead, but only a little while to love the living."

"But we don't," I said, "have all eternity to please the dead. That's the problem. If, as you say, there's no life after death, we can't make it up to them. We can't clear things up. Because you can't converse, or apologize, to someone who's dead. It's the ultimate silence. That's why people used to hold séances. That's why Mary Todd Lincoln tried to contact her son and husband that way."

"So did Harriet Beecher Stowe," she said. "So did Arthur Conan Doyle. Lots of people did—especially after World War One, when so many young men had been lost. We feel remorse. We refuse to accept the obvious fact that they cannot in any way even hear our apologies. I cannot make it up to Nick that he had to suffer and die. Nor can he see us now, talking about him."

"I think maybe he can. I think the dead can see us, too," I said. "I think you can feel them, in certain places."

"Cemeteries?" she said.

"No," I said. "Places where you were with them— places that remind you of them when you return there, the way nothing else can. Lafayette Square, in the case of Henry Adams. The house where Lincoln died. Or the Gainesville airport."

"The Gainesville airport?"

"When my sister came down to visit I used to take my mother out of the nursing home to the Gainesville airport to meet her—because when my sister came to visit, we were able to take my mother home from the nursing home for two whole weeks, because then there were two of us to care for her, and we could spell each other off. It was always a wonderful day—my mother knew she was going home for a long time, my sister was coming, we were getting a change. And my sister brought so much energy from up north. The day my mother and I went to the Gainesville airport was like Christmas when I was a child. We'd wait for my sister just inside the automatic doors where the people enter the lobby after they get off the plane. It's one of those small airports where passengers walk across the runway. My sister would come through the door and there we were, waiting. She would bend down and kiss my mother. It was so moving. Then my mother died. I avoided all the places I associated with her. I could never even drive near the nursing home. I would take long detours to avoid it—I changed doctors because his office was not far away. But last summer I had to go to the airport to rent a car. I hadn't been back in five years—but the minute I walked inside I felt everything—as if I were standing there with my mother's wheelchair tipped back so she could see through the window the moment my sister came out of the plane. All the happiness came back—and then my mother's suffering came back to me too—as if it hadn't gone away at all. And I thought: She does exist. She does exist. Where? In my heart. That's where the dead exist—in our hearts. That's where the dead are. And I learned this when I least expected it. I walked into a place I hadn't visited in five years and—at that moment I realized they really do exist—only where we cannot know."

My dead friend's mother smiled gently above the pink carnations in the vase between us, as she turned the knife over on the edge of her plate.

"But consciousness is a function of the brain," she said, "and when the brain disintegrates, as it does after death, how can there be any consciousness?"

It was like the mad calm of her son, sitting on the sofa with a blank expression on his smooth white face, because he could not understand how this had happened to someone who had been so careful about his health he had only drunk bottled water, and never gone into the sun.

"I killed my mother with boredom. She had the misfortune to become dependent on a child who was a closeted homosexual, who had kept his real life from her for years, so that when he took care of her there was nothing but him and her—no life, no family of his own, nothing but his own solitude. So every day she woke up and ate the same oatmeal and waited for me to walk in the door—me, who had no life to share with her in the first place. Every day there was only me, my isolation, my loneliness, and the routine we fell into because there was no alternative. She had the misfortune to be plunked down into my closet— where there was no air. I killed my mother with my secret and my shame. I killed her with banality."

"You didn't kill your mother!" my friend's mother said.

"She died of natural causes, from what I gather—at a perfectly ripe old age."

"I kept her alive longer than she wanted to be," I said. "The head nurse told me so. She said families often hang on to patients because they cannot let them go."

"What you are saying is that she suffered," said Mrs. Dixon.

"But never complained," I said.

"Well, that is part of love—seeing those we love suffer."

"But I was wrong not to let her go."

"Don't be absurd," she said. "Were you going to kill her?" She sighed. "Everyone feels guilty when they lose someone—they think there was something more they could have done to save them. When you can't—you can't save people from death. All you can feel guilty about is how you treated them when they were alive, as they were dying."

"That's what I'm saying," I said.

"But you took care of her as best you could! Whatever you feel you were, you did not abandon her! You are feeling guilty because you were imperfect. That's a form of snobbery. You are wallowing in guilt. The problem with guilt," she said, buttering her roll, "is that the people in life who should feel guilty don't, and the ones who shouldn't do. That's all you can say about guilt. Look at Clover Adams! She should have been proud of nursing her father till he died. Instead she felt worthless. And I suspect you're right about Mary Lincoln—she probably felt enormous guilt. She was the one who wanted her husband to be president, she was the one who wanted to go to the theater! But she survived. And so have we. But you did not kill your mother. Of course there are mothers who would like their children to think they did. It's quite possible that early in your life she made sure that you would feel that when she died," she said. "Have you considered that?"

"Yes, I have," I said. "She used to often scare me that way—she would say, 'You'll feel different when I'm dead and gone,' and things like that. She knew the words frightened me. The odd thing is that when it finally happened, so many years later, it was as if I'd never been warned. But you had something they say is worse—the death of a child, before the parent. That's what Mary Lincoln went through. That's why she resorted to séances—people believed you could contact the dead then. They had to, because they lost people so much more frequently then, to all sorts of diseases we don't need to worry about. People made fun of Mrs. Lincoln for that. Tell me. How do you account for the fact that people are affected by grief in such different degrees?"

"I think we're all set at a certain temperature," she said, "like the burner on a stove. That whatever happens to us, good or bad, we come back to the same level of happiness. As if our souls are set like a thermostat. Some people are constitutionally cheerful and others melancholy—the way the Middle Ages thought people were characterized by blood or bile. Some people are undone by grief and others get over it. But you really must decide whether you are indulging yourself or not. Plutarch told his wife not to let grief consume her after their daughter died." And then in a softer voice: "And these people are about to tell us the restaurant is closing," she said. She smiled and stood up. After saying good night to the Turkish family who ran the restaurant and walking out into the lobby, I felt again as if we were returning to our cabins on a ship my friend had taken as a child; though all we did was walk back through the tunnel, as ghoulishly lighted as the National Archives, to the building in which she lived, and say good night at the elevator.

I did not know if she expected to ever see me again or not—but for some reason (a desire to ingratiate myself, a fantasy to relieve my own predicament), I told her that I was moving permanently to Washington, as if that meant I would be there to take care of her. It occurred to me that I might take care of her, if only for my friend's sake, or my own. For now I thanked her for letting me talk to her. Then I remembered a line I'd decided to learn by heart from *Mary Todd Lincoln: Her Life and Letters* and said: "For sorrow, such as ours, there is no balm, the grave and Heaven, with reunion with our loved ones, can alone heal, bleeding, broken hearts."

And, with a little squeeze of my hand, she smiled and

got on to the elevator. I walked home in the rain and resumed reading the book: "Wherever I am, feeling so sadly, I lead a life of isolation and retirement, although I have been here several weeks, I am sure few or none are aware of it. I am not feeling sufficiently well in mind or body, to undertake Italy this winter!" The doorbell rang. I went downstairs. It was a man I'd met at the sex club who had come to tell me that he had discovered a sore on the head of his penis and may have exposed me to syphilis. I thanked him and went back upstairs. Half an hour later the doorbell rang again. A young man who said he knew my landlord and lived just a few doors down claimed he had just been in an auto accident in Dupont Circle, his wife was in the hospital, and he needed seventy dollars to get his car back from the towing company. I told him he had already tried this once before and I was not going to give him anything this time, and closed the door.

When, a few days later, I came downstairs to turn out the lights, my landlord was at the table, reading the newspaper, which he put down when I appeared. "You know," he said in a voice of childlike wonder, "I didn't sleep a wink last night. Not a wink."

"Why not?" I said.

"Oh, sometimes life becomes too plain," he said. "Especially when you can't sleep, for no good reason except anxiety."

"Anxiety about what?" I said.

"That we die in the middle of things, without any resolution, God knows where, or with whom. I mean I guess I'm wondering," he said, "how I've ended up alone."

"And what did you conclude?" I said.

"Well, it's not as if I've always been single. I had a lover," he said. "That's why I ended up in the psychiatric wing at Georgetown Hospital, twenty years ago tomorrow."

"Why?"

"Because he was unfaithful," he said. Then: "Which is putting it mildly."

"Why was he unfaithful?" I said.

"Well, he was very good-looking," he said, staring into the distance as he held his newspaper. "Everybody wanted him," he said. He returned his gaze to the *Post* and said, "And everybody had him."

Then he began laughing, straightened up, and resumed reading the paper. I went over to the table near the front door and examined the envelopes—more letters for my predecessors, men who had lived here once and now had no forwarding address: the actor, the clarinetist, the master sergeant, the activist. They'd been lying there gathering dust, the way the mail addressed to people who have died does, because to throw it out feels like admitting they have vanished; in the same way, when someone offering a magazine subscription to your mother calls, you say she is "out" or on a trip, instead of dead. But among them I saw an envelope addressed to me that bore an old-fashioned, carefully composed script—the sort only old people write anymore; it was from my neighbor in Florida, an elderly man who spent almost every day on his hands and knees under a straw hat in his yard across the street, patiently picking out weeds from his lawn.

"Good news?" my landlord said, looking up from the paper when I put the letter down.

"Yes," I said. "My house is okay. No one has broken in."

"You sound disappointed," he said, turning the page of the newspaper.

"Well, I half-wish something would happen," I said. "A bolt of lightning, a forest fire. Because I don't see how I'll leave the place otherwise. I can't imagine dispersing the contents—certainly not at a garage sale. Of course the roof is leaking, and there are carpenter ants in the beams. It just doesn't seem right to me that you should have to replace a roof—a roof, I always thought, was forever."

"Oh no," he said. "You have to replace a roof. Did you know it was leaking before you came here?"

"Yes," I said. "But I procrastinated. I'd think: I'm the only person in this house, why does it matter if the roof leaks? I'm not worth a roof." He smiled. "There are a lot of other things wrong with the house," I said, "but to have them all fixed for a single man—a man living by himself—seemed selfish."

"It's hard to live just for yourself," my landlord said, "though I know a lot of people who think like that. They go home to take care of their parents, plan to sell the house the moment they die, and then, twenty years later, they're still there," he said, turning another page, "living in Grey Gardens. You should really keep a house up. Unless you feel it's holding you back."

"From what?" I said.

"The rest of your life," he said. "You know, mortgage rates are in your favor now. They've never been lower. In fact there's a two bedroom down the street for sale—two friends of mine, as a matter of fact, who've decided they just want to spend the rest of their lives traveling."

"Hmmmm," I said.

"That doesn't sound like much of a commitment," he laughed. He turned the last page of the newspaper. "Perhaps you never will get rid of the house—and the things in it. There are lots of people like that. They die amidst their family possessions—like bag ladies."

"I just visited one," I said. "Nick Dixon's mother. She told me she could not ask me up to her apartment because it was so full of boxes she had not unpacked since moving there. I told her that's how I lived, but she still wouldn't ask me up. She also said the man in the apartment above hers had fallen and she'd had to call 911."

"Old age is awful," said my landlord. "I wonder how many people would sit down to the meal if they knew what the dessert was! Thank God we don't have to deal with that quite yet. In fact I'm invited to a party tomorrow night, some friends of mine, you're more than welcome to come. It'll be mostly lawyers and their very attractive boyfriends— in a really spectacular apartment. Another meaningless social encounter—that Washington specialty. No? Then may I ask you a favor—I won't be home till late tomorrow evening, and if it's not inconvenient, could I ask you to walk Biscuit? If you can't I can get someone else, so don't worry about it."

"I'd love to walk Biscuit," I said.

"Thanks," he said. He stood up, yawned, and turned to the mirror. "Do you like my hair like this? The guy who cuts it just did it in a new way."

"I think the way you wear it normally is better. This makes an attempt at something it shouldn't."

"Just my feeling," he said, brushing the short fringe of hair back down across his forehead, and then starting to turn out the lights We went up to our rooms like an old married couple, having darkened the house, and discussed, in the silence of night, the things that matter.


GRIEF IS LIKE Osiris; cut up in parts and thrown into the Nile. It fertilizes in ways we cannot know, the pieces of flesh bleed into every part of our lives, flooding the earth, till eventually Life appears once more. The Romans were practical: in every funeral procession there were prostitutes ready to help the mourners resume their appetitive existence. I could not tell when I stepped out of the house with the dog the next evening whether my pleasure came from doing a favor for my landlord or pretending I was he; that, for a moment, his life was mine. That's how it felt, at least, standing on N Street in the dusk waiting for the dog to sniff the flower bed in front of the house. Of course just freeing the dog was a pleasure. There was so much for her to respond to with her alertness and sensitivity outdoors, including every scrap of paper from a fast food franchise caught in the branches of the shrubs we passed along the sidewalk. She would have eaten anything, I realized—the mere memory of a hamburger. We walked down N Street to the P Street beach—a long grassy slope that led to the stream that ran through Rock Creek Park, which was still such a cruising ground for homosexuals that used condoms littered the paths and the school playground above the ravine. My landlord had warned the trail that led under the bridge along the stream was dangerous, but I went down there anyway, though I could see among the trees watching us pass a man with the same sort of gaunt, weathered face that stares out from photographs of the conspirators who had plotted to kill Lincoln and Seward. "Useless. Useless," were John Wilkes Booth's last words. That was what the face of the man in the trees seemed to be saying. I returned to the open area and ran with the dog as fast as I could. The sight of her running with such effortless speed across the grass could only give rise to thoughts of how seldom she had the opportunity to do so. A passerby asked what breed she was when we came to a stop. Then I found her nosing in someone's vomit and I put the leash back on and took her home.

The next evening there was a knock on the wall beside my door. "I just wanted to thank you for walking Biscuit," my landlord said, "I really appreciate it!"

I told him it was nothing—that she was always a pleasure. "Is everything all right up here?" he said, stepping in for the first time. "Do you know how to set the thermostat?" he said, as he looked at the needle. "Is it too warm for you at night?" I assured him everything was fine. "Well, sleep well!" he said, and went downstairs, the dog behind him. In the morning there was another thank you note on the stairs.

"That's to establish boundaries," Frank said.

The temperature in the room was too warm, in fact—I opened the windows at night until one day I felt the air conditioner come on in the house. It was spring. Crocuses and tulips were opening in the flower beds. People were starting to go out. The young man who lived with his boyfriend downstairs sat perched on the steps like a bird on the edge of its nest, reading a book, looking up from the page, looking down just in time to miss a man who had turned back to stare at him. The semester was almost over. There would be no reason to stay after the course ended; no reason I could admit, that is. My landlord meanwhile asked me one day to help string wires along the garden wall to keep the fir trees from growing into the neighbor's yard—an attorney with whom he was having a feud. Summer was coming: a season he obviously longed for. The buttercups were already blooming the day he drove me out to the Congressional Cemetery. "This is called the Gay Corner," he said, stopping at the grave of Leonard Matlovich to read aloud the words on his gravestone ("They gave me a medal for killing two men, and a discharge for loving one") and then point out, not far away, the graves of Clyde Tolson, the constant companion of J. Edgar Hoover ("They would lunch every day at the Mayflower Hotel"), and Hoover and his family. Then we walked up to the grave of Peter Doyle, Walt Whitman's bosom friend, and then to the graves of two people associated with the death of Lincoln. The first was the man who'd helped Booth escape after the assassination; he was buried in his sister's grave, since no conspirator was allowed to have his name upon a marker. The second was Lincoln's valet—the man who'd been standing outside the presidential box that night at Ford's Theatre, while the security officer was in a bar having a drink, the man who had let Booth into the box after Booth had presented his card. "And do you know what?" my landlord said. "Mary Todd Lincoln knew how the valet had loved Lincoln, and gave him the clothes Lincoln was wearing that day—not the ones in which he was killed, the ones he'd worn before they went to the play." His voice got quiet, and we stared at the grave.

At such moments, my landlord seemed like the saddest, most sensitive, of souls. As the days passed, however, and the weather became warmer, his voice seemed heartier, his laugh louder, through the open doors of the study when he talked on the phone, which only deepened my annoyance.

One evening my landlord came downstairs wearing a plastic cast of one of the breastplates Roman generals wore (something he'd bought for his store in the mountains); another night a mask. I heard music behind his bedroom doors. Another night I heard someone downstairs singing "Someone to Watch Over Me," and when I went down to investigate found a strange man sitting on the sofa. "Don't be embarrassed," I said, with a smile, as I walked down the stairs. "I'm not," he said. It was one of my landlord's friends, I realized, or a date—I could not tell—waiting for him to come down: evidence of a private life so unsettling I kept right on going and left the house.

Even the hour of my landlord's departure for work changed; he was leaving later and later. One morning on my way downstairs I bumped into him dashing across the landing stark naked. Except for the fact that his back and shoulders were now covered with a fine coat of hair and his chest now shone silver, he still had the body with which he must have attracted people in the seventies, although, as with all bodies at a certain age, it had sort of fallen in upon itself. "Oh my God!" he cried when he saw me, bending forward and covering his genitals with his hands as he laughed. He was lighthearted, he was happy, though often when he started to laugh, it was as if some relative had told him years ago not to be frivolous, because he caught himself and assumed a serious mien. Outside the deciduous magnolia was in bloom, the weeping cherry and the redbud, and even after getting dressed—late, it seemed to me, for work—he would often stop on his way to the Metro to chat with a neighbor in a puddle of pink blossoms. The nights were so cool and perfect he sat out on the stoop with Biscuit, talking to the new Swedish model who had moved into a house five doors away. In summer, he'd told me, he went to a public pool five minutes away popular with young gay men, and, refusing to be intimidated, "I just waddle right out there and dive in." He was going to enjoy a season I'd never seen in Washington—summer; which seemed to have been inaugurated by the water the city had turned on in Dupont Circle, now falling past the voluptuous caryatids that held up the fountain's large flat bowl. At night I listened with increasing irritation to the laughter beyond the study doors he no longer bothered to close, as if he had no secrets from me.

"It's because you're leaving," Frank said when I met

him in the Circle one evening at his request. He'd spent all day in doctors' offices having tests run and did not want to return home just yet. He glanced to both sides before removing from the pocket of his pants a single cigarette. "Intimacy is now possible because you're going," he said. "He's returning you to the status you had when you came—hence the thank you note. It's just as well, I suppose. You mustn't attach yourself to places or people like that. The average American moves twelve times in his life. So get with it! For example, the Lug and I are going to Cape Cod Friday and and I was wondering if I could ask you to do me a favor. Would you walk over and feed Sammy? And make sure there's water in his bowl? He hardly eats anything anymore he's so old, and I wouldn't be surprised if he croaked when I'm gone, but I've just got to get away. I'd really appreciate it."

"Of course," I said.

"Thanks," he said. "That's something single people can do, you know—pet sit. You have to do something—because I see you with a good twenty years left. They may not all be good ones, but I see you with at least twenty more."

"Is that how you see people?" I said. "With how many years they have left?"

"That's exactly how I see them," he said. "The number might as well be tattooed on their foreheads."

"Because you're so conscious of your own," I said.

"That's right," he said. "You think Love is hard to find.

Try finding a cure for cancer! The doctor tells me I have a forty percent chance of recurrence. That's why I'm looking forward to this summer," he went on, stretching his arms out. "I'm going to padlock myself to this bench— and eat ice cream all day long! With you beside me," he said, looking over at me. "Showing off your gams in a pair of hot pants, and those wonderful deltoids you've been developing at the gym! You have to stay here, you see. I need you. It's for your own sake, too. You can't go back to that house and what you were, even though I know you'd like to. Everybody wants to hide, but you can't let yourself."

We said good-bye, and I went home. Sitting in the living room watching the man in the plaid jacket pick leaves off the sidewalk one by one, I tried to think of something to say to my last class—a valedictory of sorts, the benefit of everything I'd thought and felt about Life—a warning, in essence, that whether your husband was assassinated beside you as you sat watching a third-rate play, or you tripped on a rug and broke your neck, or were infected in a moment of sexual passion (or boredom, or loneliness) by a fatal virus, life had a way of suddenly flipping, and that something, sometime, somewhere, almost certainly would flip it for them, to one degree or another—but I decided it would all sound morbid, and I brought the class to a close the next day with a flurry of practical references to the length and due date of their final projects, and the seminar ended on an anticlimactic note.

With that I started down Cathedral Avenue in the gathering dark—past the huge apartment building in which my dead friend's mother lived, past the bus shelter in front of it, where I found the visiting poet hunched over a hero sandwich in a light rain, having dinner by himself, past the Vice President's residence where there was nothing but the darkness of the fir trees and men in black circling on their bicycles, and then Sheridan Circle, and then Dupont, which, on a warm spring night, once the rain had stopped, was swarming with people, sitting out at sidewalk cafés in the ghoulish radiance of the crime-retardant streetlights, like figures in a shabby Paris. Then the house, from which I was detaching already, and the decline of Mary Todd Lincoln. I was nearing the end of the book. She had already been judged insane at the trial instigated by her son Robert in Chicago, a verdict she had protested by attempting to poison herself in the hotel lobby afterward, after going up and down Wabash Avenue trying to buy laudanum at various drugstores from already alerted pharmacists who substituted sugar for the powder she requested. As soon as she was released from her confinement she went to New York. Her last letter, from there, was dated March 21, 1882. I could barely bring myself to read it. She was staying at the Grand Central Hotel after having received treatments earlier at Miller's Hotel on West Twenty-third Street in their "Turkish, Electric and Roman baths." She was losing her eyesight, and so lame she could hardly walk, and was still obsessed with obtaining an increase in her pension from Congress, suspicious of everyone, alienated from her only surviving son, after he'd had her committed, not even trusting her old friends, about to board a train that would take her up the Hudson River, to Buffalo, Cleveland, and Toledo, and finally her sister's house in Springfield, Illinois, the house in which she had been married.

"I dread the journey greatly, with my limbs still in so paralyzed a state—" was the last line she wrote, I told Frank when I met him in Dupont Circle later that night to get his keys.

"But that's just how I feel about traveling!" he said. "Especially with the Lug!"

He looked around to see if anyone nearby would see him taking out his pack of cigarettes, for fear he would come over and ask him for a smoke. Since there was a man nearby who looked as if he were waiting to do just that, we stopped talking altogether, while Frank folded his hands in his lap. Finally the man walked away. Then Frank lighted a cigarette and said: "You know, you really have to ask yourself why you're obsessing on this woman. I have three theories. One, you're grieving and that's, from what you tell me, what she apparently did the rest of her life after the White House. Two, you get to feel sorry for someone who was worse off than you—which is the use we eventually put most of our public figures to. And three—she reminds you of your mother! And so," he said, his voice rising, "for that matter, does your landlord's dog!"

I said that was nonsense; I felt sorry for the dog because he left her there all day, sometimes into the night, and she was all alone, and had no power of her own to go in or out, and was basically stuck in that room till someone opened the door to let her out.

"What have you just given a perfect description of?"

"Mary Todd Lincoln in a hotel in Frankfurt?"

"An old woman in a nursing home—waiting for her son to visit!" he said. "Believe me, I know. Only mine didn't recognize me, which made it easier not to go. You're still wishing you could go to the nursing home and feed your mother dinner!"

"How could anyone wish that?"

"Because you felt useful! And loved! You've never had such an experience of intimacy—or been able to be selfless—thereby wiping out the guilt you carry for being gay! You don't have to tell me about it. I've been there, dear."

"Not quite," I said.

"What do you mean?" Frank said.

"Because there are things I haven't told you," I said. "One is that my mother asked me to bring her home for good just before she died. She knew she was dying, I realize now, but I of course was mired in my routine and didn't want to even contemplate her disappearance. I *was* happy, in a strange way, I see now—for all the reasons you just pointed out. So when she said she didn't have long and asked if I wouldn't bring her home for good, I said nothing, thinking she was being melodramatic. And then she died just when she said she would. In other words, I refused her the one thing we all want—to die in our own bed, amidst our own things, and not with strangers. That's why people don't want to die in prison, you know. That's why I'm afraid to fly. Nobody wants to die with strangers. If I had known, of course, I would have gotten Hospice and brought her home. But I didn't know, or I didn't want to know, because I could not bear the idea of her dying. She'd teased us when we were children, as mothers do, with the threat of her death. Then it happened. And I refused to bring her home when she knew she was dying. Like Robert Lincoln, putting Mary Todd in the insane asylum. He thought it was for the best, too, and one can see why he did it. But it was wrong."

"The gift of hindsight!" said Frank.

"But there's something else," I said. "The last thing she said to me—we were at home, for the weekend. She was so weak she could hardly hold her head up, you could see Death pressing her down, almost physically. I had just hung up the phone, after talking to you. She had asked me before why only men called me, and I had always made up some explanation. But this time when I hung up the phone she said—'Are you homosexual?' It was the one thing that would have explained everything. Instead I walked out of the room—because I didn't want to give her that power—

of knowing I was. But I see now she had every right to have that admitted. I was her work, after all."

"And that's what's been bothering you?" he said.

"Yes," I said.

He rolled his eyes. "Must I remind you of what I told you the first week you were here?" he said.

"What?"

"The dead don't care whether you're homosexual! Whether you think of the dead, or grieve, or visit their grave, or wish they were still alive, or could accept your apologies, or know you feel remorse—they're not registering any of it! You can't apologize to the dead, and you can't love them, because—they're dead! Unconscious! Decomposed! Disintegrated! Done!"

I looked down at the ground. "You don't think they're watching us at all?" I said.

"No!" he said. "And I don't think your landlord's dog is your mother! I think his dog is *you*—going back to that house, waiting for dark to take your walk, living there by yourself—instead of moving here." He stood up. "I know it's tough to find love. And sometimes a dog is all we can manage. But at a certain point one makes the leap to—humans. Sorry, I'm all out," he smiled at a man who had come up to him to ask for a cigarette. "Now don't forget to make sure there's water in the dish," he said, turning to me.

"I won't. I haven't forgotten something else you said, either," I said. "Remember when you said you were afraid the Lug would leave you? Well, what you were afraid of didn't happen. You weren't abandoned."

"No," he said. "Not by the Lug. But Sammy is dying, and that may be worse." He looked at the fountain. As big and handsome as he was, he seemed at that moment to shrink in his baggy pants and old sweatshirt. "He's been with me for sixteen years," he said, his blond hair gleaming in the streetlight coming from the outer edges of the park. "He's been with me every place I've lived since I got back from Europe. I can't imagine him not being there. But he's old. And he's dying. So be gentle with him. And thanks. I appreciate it," he said, and walked off.

"Hey, bro, how's it goin'?" said the man who had been refused the opportunity to ask for a cigarette. He was dirty and begrimed, like a coal miner, and he stank, like the mulch that had been put in the flower beds all around town, but for a moment I thought: This is what Mary Todd Lincoln was doing all those years after the assassination—refusing to pretend that she had a home on earth, advertising the fact that she did not by always wearing black, a custom no one observes anymore—and I thought of what she must have felt the day she left the White House, how bereft, how bitter, while Grant and Johnson were reviewing a military parade in the street nearby. After someone you love dies, you are homeless, really, because your home was once with them. The dead *are* watching. The homeless around me in Dupont Circle were like Mary

Todd Lincoln in widow's weeds: advertising their refusal. I left them in the park, however, and went back to the comfort and quiet of my landlord's house.

To my consternation it was empty. On Sunday I left to feed Frank's cat. The downstairs tenant's boyfriend was sitting on the steps reading when I went out. He was about thirty but looked sixteen. He had dark brown hair and perfect features; an upturned nose, long-lashed eyes, and a shock of dark glossy brown hair, cut like a schoolkid's, or an English choirboy singing matins in the depths of some cathedral—perched on the steps like an animal that has come out of its burrow to sniff the air but is not going to stray far in case it has to run back quickly. He kept lifting his head from his book to look at the street. Then the breeze would turn one of the pages of his book, and he would look down, flatten the page, and resume reading, so that he failed every time to see the person pass by who turned to look back at him. Moments later he'd look up again, just missing another admirer.

Evidently he did not really want to read—though when I went out, and he heard the door opening behind him, his head bobbed down again until I said hello. We talked about the weather, what he was reading, Washington; he asked me about the Eagle, a bar his lover would not allow him to visit, school, my home. I said I was going across Dupont Circle to feed a friend's cat that might be dead. He offered to go with me. It was so early the only people in Dupont Circle were the men I'd left the night before, still in their sleeping bags on the benches. P Street was empty. The cat was nowhere to be seen till I went into the bedroom and found him on the bed, his face folded into his paws. When I woke him he blinked, with an irritated expression, as if he had been awakened from a long, drugged sleep. I carried him to the kitchen, put his food in a bowl, and then went into the living room. My companion stood at the bookcase reading the titles. Then I returned to the kitchen, lifted the cat from its bowl, and put it back on the bed. It was so soft it seemed to have no bones at all. When we let ourselves out of the apartment we stole one last glance at the poor animal on the bed.

My landlord was asleep too, on the sofa downstairs, the newspaper fallen from his hands, the dog on the floor at his feet. I stood there looking at him while the dog looked up at me. Spring filled the house: the doors to the garden were open, the white petals of some flowering tree had drifted in across the golden floor. There was a fresh bunch of lavender tulips on the dining room table and the curtains in the front windows had been changed from the gauzy silver stuff that looked almost like panty hose to a more tropical-looking set of bamboo shades, which, as if they had now set the tone, had induced my landlord to put on the khaki shorts and Top-Siders with no socks he was wearing now. "Hi, sport," he said, opening his eyes the way some people do after a nap, without apparently being aware he had been unconscious. "Did you get the message about the cat?"

"I just fed it," I said, "although it's very old, I don't know how it's still alive."

"I ask myself the same thing," he said. He sat up. "That's how I want to die. I just want to fall asleep."

I told him the downstairs tenant's boyfriend had gone with me.

"He's a sweetheart," he said. "How's his other half?"

"I guess okay," I said. "I haven't seen him lately."

"Well, I haven't spoken to him in years."

"Why not?" I said.

"Because he's the man who put me in the loony bin at Georgetown," he said. "Twenty years ago."

"Ah," I said.

"But by then he owned part of the house," he said. "I let him buy in when we were a couple. Then the divorce, but neither of us wished to sell. Since this had become home for both of us. Then he had a small problem with cocaine and had to sell his share to me—and now he rents downstairs with his new lover. What can you do? Everybody needs a home." He looked up at me and smiled.

"Funny—I was just thinking—that's what Mrs. Lincoln never found," I said.

"No, she didn't."

"And that was her problem. She thought life was over," I said.

"It was," he said.

"But she was still alive," I said.

"Well, that *was* the problem. But I don't think she was unreasonable to feel the way she did. Sometimes you should admit your life's behind you!" he said, stretching his arms. "That you're simply trying to make what remains as unirritating as possible. That you can never be happy again. That's why she never went back to her sister's house—the house in which she was married—until she had no choice—and even then she slept on only one side of the bed, leaving the other half for Lincoln, lying there in a dark room with just one candle burning because her eyes were so sensitive to light, while outside in the street the neighborhood kids played games and made fun of the crazy lady. Have you finished the book yet?" he said.

"I just did," I said.

"All those dashes and exclamation points!" he said, picking the book up. He opened it where I'd left the bookmark, and began reading. "A fearful cold, appeared to settle in my spine and I was unable to sit up, with the sharp, burning agony, in my back. I have now a plaster from my shoulders down the whole, extent of the spine and I am lying on my sofa most of the time—The doctor says, this present trouble arises more from a distressed agitated mind, than a real local cause, but says of course there is a great tendency to spinal disease—You can imagine or rather you cannot— but I have lived through this recent time, with only a grim faced landlady, to look in upon me, once in a few hours. I often think I must be invisible supported, loving ones must be watching over me in silence and it can be BUT grief, to see me so desolate and lonely and at times so very helpless— Tomorrow is the anniversary of my precious husband's birthday—and it may be if my health continues to fail me as it now is so fast doing, another birthday may find me with him."

"Have you ever," he said, closing the book, "read such an insane mixture of self-pity, melodrama, camp, and real grief? She rings all the chimes! From a figure whose tragedy no one in American history could match to a conniving, paranoid shopaholic!"

"Because she never moved on," I said. "She would not let herself—she was faithful to the end to Lincoln. Love *is* eternal. She mourned. And what is the point of mourning? What does it accomplish? Just this—faithfulness. And love."

He fell silent for a moment and watched some people passing by on the street stop and point up to his bay window.

"You know, that apartment I told you about down the block is still for sale—the one owned by the two guys who plan to spend the rest of their lives traveling. You should take a look," he said. "People never say anything nice about Washington, but I think you'd agree with me—you can have one nice day here after another." He stood up. "But now I'm off to meet a young man who wants to rent the room—he's moving down from New York to fund-

raise for the Holocaust Museum—another cheerful subject! If you leave before I get up tomorrow, sport, just put
the keys through the mail slot."

Why he was calling me "sport" I had no idea. The dog
at his side was watching me with her usual alert expression,
but she made no move to come to me; I, who had liberated
her so many mornings and afternoons. Ears up, mouth
open, she was on her way with her master—she was going
on a trip. They were a unit, the two of them: she belonged
to him.

THE MINUTE THEY were out the door I went upstairs and
put the book back where I'd found it, between the two glass
bookends. Then I picked up my books and papers, removed all my clothes from the hangers in the closet, and
packed my bags. By the time I'd finished, the room looked
exactly as it had the day I arrived. So, I thought, it was just
a commercial transaction after all—like so much in this
country. In the bathroom I scraped the gluey soap off the
soap dish and made sure there was not a hair on the porce-
lain or any trace of my having been there. Then I lay down
on the bed and watched the light in the room change, just as
I had the day of my arrival. I could scarcely believe I was
about to leave. The hours passed. It was dusk when I arose.
Then I went downstairs to take one last walk, stopping first
before the mirror. The lighting was different now that it

was spring—much brighter. You're leaving, my reflection said, you're leaving this city with all the people, the fountains and museums and walks. You're going back—back to an empty house—for a reason you don't even understand. Furious, I went down the stairs.

The city had never looked lovelier—to my chagrin. Looking down Massachusetts Avenue the general on the horse surrounded by blossoming cherry trees in the center of Scott Circle seemed to be fording a surf composed entirely of pink foam. The dogwood and redbud were still in bloom on the walk between the White House and the Treasury Building. Then the tall trees, about to come into leaf, around the monument to General Sherman, and then the dull Ellipse, and then the Mall. It was late in the day, and people were going home, with glum expressions on their faces, and it was only when I'd started up the slope toward the Washington Monument that I felt the curious lifting of the spirit one always gets at that moment, like a child about to fly a kite. Then I turned left onto the long alley of the Mall itself, and passed some of the dusty families retreating from the Air and Space Museum, and two Marines, their faces bleached with sweat, ecstatic with exertion, as they jogged down the gravel path.

It was spring, but it was still cold, and in the center of the Mall huge clouds of vapor rose from the heating vents, on which homeless men lay wrapped in sleeping bags. A sliver of an early moon hung like a scimitar above the roof of the

Smithsonian as I sat there watching the trees darken to silhouettes, and the hard white marble of the Capitol soften against the pale blue sky. Then the planes landing at National Airport switched on their headlights, like automobiles, while the homeless men lying nearby on their piles of blankets argued over the relative merits of the city's emergency rooms, like people rating four-star restaurants, one of them as young, blond, and handsome as Billy Budd. What had brought him there? What was his story? I didn't ask. Instead I sat there thinking one of the figures coming toward me on the gravel walk might be the love of my life.

The next morning I left the city in one of the blue vans that constantly circulate its streets, taking people to the airports like cells that remove free radicals from the blood. On the sidewalks we passed were handsome men in dark suits and ties. The plane ride back reminded me of the plane ride up: a sepulchral silence, everyone once more a total stranger.

The minute I entered the house, my grief returned; and I fell to my knees between my parents' beds with a deep gratitude and said a prayer: Thank you, God, for bringing me home safely. Blessed be the Lord, bless my father and mother.